CHARLES VANCE

MQTT Systems Made Easy

This book was professionally typeset on Reedsy.
Find out more at reedsy.com

Contents

1

Chapter 1: Introduction

Purpose of the Book

"Building MQTT Systems Made Easy" is designed to be a comprehensive guide for developers, engineers, and enthusiasts looking to delve into the world of real-time messaging using MQTT and JSON, particularly within the Python programming environment. The primary goal of this book is to equip you with the practical knowledge and skills required to design, build, and maintain efficient MQTT systems capable of handling JSON-formatted data.

Scope of the Book

The book covers a wide range of topics necessary to fully understand and implement MQTT and JSON in Python:

- **Fundamental Concepts**: You'll start with the basics, gaining a solid understanding of MQTT as a messaging protocol and JSON as a data format. This includes exploring how these technologies fit into the larger landscape of networked applications and IoT solutions.
- **Technical Skills**: The chapters progress into more technical details,

teaching you how to set up MQTT brokers and clients, handle JSON data efficiently in Python, and integrate these components into cohesive applications.

- **Advanced Techniques**: As you advance, the book introduces more complex scenarios, including secure messaging, optimizing communication for scalability and reliability, and employing advanced features like Quality of Service (QoS) levels and persistent sessions.
- **Practical Applications**: Practical case studies and examples throughout the book demonstrate how MQTT and JSON can be applied to real-world situations, such as home automation, industrial monitoring, and IoT device management.

Main Themes

- **MQTT**: Dive into the world of MQTT to understand its lightweight structure and its suitability for environments where network bandwidth is at a premium. Learn how to establish and manage connections, publish and subscribe to topics, and ensure message security.
- **JSON**: Explore JSON's role as a flexible and widely-used data format in modern applications, focusing on its integration with Python. Learn to parse, generate, and manipulate JSON data, ensuring your applications can effectively communicate and exchange data.
- **Python Applications**: Python serves as the backbone for programming concepts in this book. You will use Python to interact with MQTT protocols and handle JSON data, leveraging Python's robust libraries and frameworks.

By the end of this book, you should be proficient in building and deploying robust MQTT systems that efficiently handle JSON data, ensuring you are well-equipped to tackle projects in various scales and complexities in the realm of networked applications and IoT.

Who Should Read This Book

Whether you are a seasoned developer, a student, or simply an enthusiast eager to explore the possibilities of MQTT and JSON, this book offers valuable insights and practical skills. Here's a breakdown of the target audience for whom this book will be particularly beneficial:

Software Developers

- **Experienced Developers**: For those already familiar with Python or other programming languages, this book provides a deep dive into real-time messaging protocols, helping you expand your skill set into IoT and network communication.
- **Aspiring Developers**: If you are relatively new to programming or looking to specialize in a growing field, this book offers a structured and clear introduction to essential concepts in networking, data handling, and IoT implementations.

IoT Enthusiasts

- **Professionals in IoT**: For individuals working in industries that rely on IoT technologies, such as home automation, healthcare, manufacturing, and smart cities, this book teaches how to implement efficient, secure, and scalable messaging systems.
- **Hobbyists**: Even if your interest in IoT is not professional, this book provides the tools to start building your own projects, such as automating your home environment or creating custom devices that interact through the internet.

Students

- **Undergraduate and Graduate Students**: Students pursuing degrees in computer science, engineering, or related fields will find this book especially useful for understanding and applying concepts in real-time data exchange and IoT, which are increasingly important in the tech industry.

- **Self-Learners**: Those engaged in self-directed learning can use this book as a resource to gain practical skills and theoretical knowledge in a structured way, preparing for careers in technology or just satisfying personal curiosity.

Tech Industry Professionals

- **System Architects and Network Engineers**: For those involved in designing and maintaining scalable systems, this book provides practical guidance on using MQTT and JSON within large-scale operations, ensuring robust and efficient data flow.

This book aims to be an accessible yet thorough guide, whether you're looking to implement professional solutions, enhance your academic understanding, or simply explore new technologies for personal projects. It offers step-by-step instructions and real-world examples to ensure all readers gain a strong grasp of the topics discussed.

How to Use This Book

It's important to approach the material with a structured strategy, especially considering the technical nature of the topics. Here's how you can effectively navigate this book, whether you're using it for self-study, as part of a course, or as a reference in your professional work.

Prerequisite Knowledge

Before diving into this book, having a basic understanding of the following areas will greatly enhance your learning experience:

- **Python Programming**: Familiarity with Python syntax and basic programming concepts such as loops, functions, and classes is essential, as the examples and projects in the book are Python-based.

- **General Networking Concepts**: An understanding of basic networking principles such as TCP/IP, client-server model, and the concept of APIs will be helpful.
- **Basic Understanding of Web Technologies**: Knowledge of how web technologies work including HTTP protocols and web sockets can be beneficial, although not strictly necessary.

Structured Reading

- **Sequential Approach**: For beginners, it is recommended to read the book sequentially, as each chapter builds upon the knowledge of the previous one.
- **Modular Approach**: If you are already familiar with some aspects of MQTT or JSON, you may choose to focus on specific chapters or sections that are most relevant to your needs.

Hands-On Practice

- **Code Along**: Try to code along with the examples provided in the book. Practicing alongside reading is one of the best ways to understand and remember the concepts.
- **Exercises and Projects**: At the end of each chapter, engage with the exercises and projects to reinforce the material covered. These practical tasks are designed to challenge your understanding and encourage you to apply what you've learned in real-world scenarios.

Supplementary Resources

- **Official Documentation**: Refer to the official Python, MQTT, and JSON documentation for more detailed and advanced topics.
- **Online Courses and Tutorials**: Augment your learning with online

courses on Python, MQTT, and IoT from platforms like Coursera, Udemy, or YouTube.

- **Community Forums**: Participate in communities such as Stack Overflow, Reddit, or technology-specific forums where you can ask questions, share knowledge, and learn from the experiences of others.

Professional Application

- **Reference Material**: Use this book as a reference guide when working on projects related to MQTT or IoT in your professional environment.
- **Stay Updated**: The field of technology is always evolving. Use this book as a foundation, but stay updated with the latest developments in MQTT, JSON, and Python through blogs, articles, and official documentation updates.

By following this approach, readers from various backgrounds can effectively engage with the book's content, making complex topics in MQTT and JSON approachable and actionable. Whether you are a student, a hobbyist, or a professional, this book aims to provide you with both the theoretical knowledge and practical skills necessary to excel in the field of real-time internet messaging.

What is MQTT?

MQTT, or Message Queuing Telemetry Transport, is a lightweight messaging protocol that excels in environments where network resources are constrained or where systems require reliable message delivery over potentially unreliable networks. Initially developed in 1999 by Andy Stanford-Clark (IBM) and Arlen Nipper (Arcom, now Eurotech), MQTT has become a standard in the IoT (Internet of Things) space due to its simplicity, efficiency, and robust feature set.

Key Features of MQTT

- **Lightweight Protocol**: MQTT is designed to be bandwidth-efficient, making it ideal for scenarios where network capacity is limited, such as in remote locations or on mobile devices.
- **Publish-Subscribe Model**: Unlike traditional client-server models, MQTT uses a publish-subscribe pattern. This means that clients publish messages to a broker, and other clients subscribe to topics to receive those messages. This model decouples message senders and receivers, providing more flexible network architectures.
- **Reliability and Quality of Service (QoS)**: MQTT offers three levels of QoS to cater to different reliability needs:
- **QoS 0 (At Most Once)**: The message is delivered at most once, and delivery is not confirmed.
- **QoS 1 (At Least Once)**: The message is guaranteed to be delivered at least once. The broker or client will attempt delivery until an acknowledgment is received.
- **QoS 2 (Exactly Once)**: The highest level, ensuring that each message is received only once by the counterpart. It's achieved through a four-step handshake process, making it the most reliable, but also the most resource-consuming option.
- **Low Power Usage**: MQTT is suitable for devices running on battery or limited power sources, as it requires minimal power for data transmission and can support intermittent connections.
- **Last Will and Testament (LWT)**: A feature that allows clients to notify other clients about an unplanned disconnection, which is crucial for monitoring the health of connected devices.

Ideal Use Cases

- **IoT and Home Automation**: Due to its efficient message delivery system and minimal bandwidth usage, MQTT is widely used in home automation systems and IoT applications where multiple devices need to communicate seamlessly.

- **Telemetry**: Originally designed for telemetry, MQTT is perfect for transmitting data from sensors and other monitoring devices in real-time, even over unstable or low-bandwidth networks.
- **Vehicle Tracking and Fleet Management**: The lightweight nature of MQTT makes it suitable for tracking vehicles in real-time, where constant connection quality cannot be guaranteed.

Why MQTT in Modern Applications?

The simplicity and efficiency of MQTT make it particularly appealing for modern applications that rely on real-time data exchange. Its ability to maintain high levels of performance and reliability under challenging network conditions, paired with its support for secure communication, ensures that it remains a preferred choice for developers working on applications ranging from simple home automation to complex industrial systems.

MQTT stands out as a highly effective protocol for scenarios demanding efficient, reliable, and scalable messaging solutions across various industries, particularly where connectivity might be intermittent or limited.

What is JSON?

JSON, which stands for JavaScript Object Notation, is a lightweight data-interchange format that is easy for humans to read and write, and simple for machines to parse and generate. Developed in the early 2000s by Douglas Crockford, it was designed as an alternative to XML and other heavier data formats primarily for web applications, but its utility has expanded far beyond that.

Characteristics of JSON

- **Text-Based and Language-Independent**: JSON is text, and while it uses conventions that are familiar to programmers of the C-family of languages, including C, C++, Java, JavaScript, Perl, Python, and others, it is language-independent. This makes JSON an ideal data format for cross-language applications.
- **Human-Readable**: The format is self-describing and easy to understand, which simplifies the job of writing code to interact with JSON data.
- **Hierarchical**: JSON can represent data hierarchically (objects containing arrays, and arrays containing objects), making it a versatile choice for complex data structures.

Structure of JSON

JSON is built on two structures:

- **Objects**: An object in JSON is an unordered set of name/value pairs. An object begins with { (left brace) and ends with } (right brace). Each name is followed by : (colon) and the name/value pairs are separated by , (comma).
- **Arrays**: An array is an ordered collection of values. An array begins with [(left bracket) and ends with] (right bracket). Values are separated by , (comma).

Here's a simple example:

```
{
  "name": "John Doe",
  "age": 30,
  "isEmployed": true,"address": {
    "street": "1234 Elm St",
    "city": "Somewhere"
  },"phoneNumbers": ["123-456-7890", "456-789-0123"]
}
```

Role in Data Interchange

JSON's format allows it to be easily sent and received over networks, making it particularly well-suited for web APIs and configurations:

- **Web APIs**: Many web services use JSON to provide public data feeds. It's commonly used in REST APIs and web services to send data between clients and servers, web applications, and databases due to its lightweight nature and ability to quickly parse large amounts of data.
- **Configuration Files**: JSON is often used in configuration files of modern programming frameworks. It provides a straightforward way to store and transmit configuration settings.

Advantages Over Other Formats

Compared to XML, another popular data-interchange format, JSON is more compact, less verbose, and quicker to read and write. This makes it particularly useful in web applications where bandwidth and performance are concerns. JSON's format also maps directly to data structures used in most programming languages, simplifying code implementation and reducing the need for extensive parsing and translations.

Today, JSON is widely regarded as the standard for data interchange on the web, particularly for client-server communications. Its simplicity, coupled with its robust capability to structure complex data, makes it indispensable in modern programming and application development. JSON continues to play a critical role in data interchange across many programming environments, making it a fundamental skill for developers.

Definition and Significance of Real-Time Messaging in Modern Applications

Definition of Real-Time Messaging

Real-time messaging refers to the instantaneous transmission of data between devices or systems without perceptible delay. In this context, "real-time" means that as events or data are generated, they are immediately communicated and processed, enabling immediate responses or actions based on the latest information.

Significance in Modern Applications

Real-time messaging is increasingly crucial across a range of industries, particularly those where timely data is pivotal for operational efficiency, safety, and decision-making. Its significance is underscored in several key sectors:

Oil and Gas

In the oil and gas industry, real-time messaging facilitates the monitoring and management of extensive pipeline networks, offshore rigs, and onshore wells. The ability to instantly receive data about pressure changes, flow rates, and equipment status allows for rapid response to potential leaks, failures, or hazardous conditions, significantly reducing environmental risks and operational costs.

Agriculture

Precision agriculture relies heavily on real-time messaging to optimize resources and crop yields. Sensors distributed throughout farms can send immediate updates on soil moisture, nutrient levels, and crop health to centralized management systems. This data enables farmers to make instant decisions about irrigation, fertilization, and harvesting, ensuring that resources are used efficiently and crops are managed optimally.

Discrete Manufacturing

In discrete manufacturing environments, such as automotive or electronics production, real-time messaging systems ensure that machinery and assembly lines operate synchronously and efficiently. Immediate communication of system statuses and production metrics helps in identifying bottlenecks, preventing equipment failures, and maintaining continuous production flow, which are essential for meeting production targets and maintaining quality standards.

Industrial Automation

Real-time messaging is the backbone of industrial automation, enabling devices, sensors, and systems to communicate seamlessly within the Industrial Internet of Things (IIoT). This integration allows for automated processes to adjust to changing conditions without human intervention, enhancing efficiency, and reducing downtime.

Supply Chain and Logistics

In logistics, real-time messaging systems track the location and condition of goods as they move through supply chains. Instant alerts about delays, environmental conditions, or route changes help companies to dynamically adjust logistics plans, reduce waste, and improve delivery times.

Energy Sector

For energy providers, especially in renewable sectors like wind and solar, real-time data messaging is crucial for balancing supply and demand. Instant data on production levels and energy consumption helps manage grid stability and optimize energy distribution, crucial for maintaining reliability in renewable energy supplies.

The critical importance of real-time messaging in these sectors cannot be overstated. It not only supports enhanced operational efficiency and safety but also drives significant cost savings and environmental benefits by enabling more precise control over industrial processes. As industries continue to evolve towards more interconnected and automated systems, the role of real-time messaging will only grow, becoming a fundamental element in the digital transformation of industries worldwide.

2

Chapter 2: JSON

Definition and Overview of JSON

JSON (JavaScript Object Notation) is a lightweight data-interchange format that is easy for humans to read and write, as well as simple for machines to parse and generate. Initially developed in the early 2000s by Douglas Crockford, JSON has become a ubiquitous format in modern web and application development, largely due to its straightforwardness and efficiency.

Role as a Data-Interchange Format

JSON serves as a bridge between systems by providing a standardized method to represent structured data in a text format, which can be easily transmitted across network connections. Here are several key aspects of JSON's role as a data-interchange format:

- **Platform Independent**: JSON is a text format that is completely language-independent. It uses conventions familiar to programmers of many languages, including C, C++, Java, JavaScript, Perl, Python, and more. This universality makes JSON an ideal choice for data interchange across heterogeneous systems.

- **Human Readable**: JSON is designed for human readability and ease of use. Its structure—objects (key/value pairs) and arrays (ordered lists)—mirrors the way data is organized in most programming languages, making it intuitive for developers to understand and manipulate.
- **Lightweight**: Compared to other data-interchange formats like XML, JSON is less verbose and less complex, which translates to quicker parsing and reduced data overhead when transmitting over networks. This makes it particularly well-suited for internet applications and services where bandwidth may be limited or data transfer speeds are critical.
- **Flexibility**: JSON can represent simple data structures and associative arrays (called objects), making it highly flexible to model complex data suitable for a wide variety of applications beyond web development, including configuration files, data serialization, and messaging for IoT protocols like MQTT.

JSON's simplicity, readability, and language-independence contribute significantly to its widespread adoption as a preferred format for data interchange, particularly in environments where minimal overhead and maximum speed are required.

Syntax Rules for Writing JSON

JSON (JavaScript Object Notation) is designed with a simple and clear syntax that makes it easy to represent data as structured text. Understanding the basic syntax rules is essential for anyone working with JSON, whether it's for configuring systems, coding applications, or interfacing with web APIs. Here's an overview of the primary syntax components in JSON:

Objects

- **Structure**: JSON objects are written inside curly braces {}. They are composed of key/value pairs, where each key is a string (enclosed in double quotes), followed by a colon :, and then the value associated with that key.
- **Example**:

```
{
  "name": "John",
  "age": 30,
  "isStudent": false
}
```

Arrays

- **Structure**: JSON arrays are written inside square brackets []. An array contains a list of values, which can be numbers, strings, objects, arrays, booleans, or null. The values in an array are separated by commas.
- **Example**:

```
["apple", "banana", "cherry"]
```

Values

- JSON values can be:
- **String**: A sequence of zero or more Unicode characters, wrapped in double quotes. Example: "Hello World"
- **Number**: An integer or floating point. Example: 123 or 19.99
- **Object**: An unordered set of key
- pairs. Example: { "firstName": "John", "lastName": "Doe" }
- **Array**: An ordered list of values. Example: [1, 2, 3, 4]
- **Boolean**: True or false values. Example: true or false
- **Null**: An empty value. Example: null

Key/Value Pairs in Objects

- **Keys** must always be strings and be enclosed in double quotes.
- **Values** in key/value pairs can be any JSON data type.
- **Separators**: Each key/value pair is separated from the next by a comma.

Nested Structures

- JSON supports complex data structures through nesting, where arrays and objects can be nested within each other.
- **Example of Nested JSON:**

```
{
  "name": "John",
  "age": 30,
  "contactDetails": {
    "email": "john@example.com",
    "phoneNumbers": ["123-456-7890", "456-789-0123"]
    },
  "hobbies": ["reading", "games", "hiking"]
}
```

No Comments Allowed

- Unlike some other data formats, JSON does not support comments. Including comments in a JSON file will lead to errors during parsing.

By adhering to these syntax rules, JSON data can be correctly formatted and easily shared between different systems, applications, and services, ensuring interoperability and consistency in data exchange.

Data Types Supported by JSON

JSON (JavaScript Object Notation) supports a limited set of data types, which are universally understood across various programming languages. This simplicity is one of the reasons why JSON is so popular for data interchange. Here are the primary data types supported by JSON:

Strings

- **Definition**: Strings in JSON are sequences of zero or more Unicode characters. JSON strings are enclosed in double quotes.
- **Example**: "Hello, world!"

Numbers

- **Definition**: JSON numbers can be integers or floating-point numbers. There is no distinction between different types of numbers in JSON; there are no separate types for integers and floats.
- **Example**: 42 or 3.14159
- **Note**: JSON does not support numeric formats like NaN or Infinity; they are typically represented as null or strings.

Objects

- **Definition**: An object in JSON is an unordered set of key/value pairs (also known as a dictionary or hash in some programming languages). Objects are enclosed in curly braces {}, with each key followed by a colon : and the key/value pairs separated by commas.

Arrays

- **Definition**: Arrays are ordered collections of values, which can be of any data type. Arrays in JSON are enclosed in square brackets [] and the values are separated by commas.
- **Example**: [1, "two", 3.0, true]

5. Booleans

- **Definition**: JSON supports the two boolean values true and false.
- **Example**: true

6. Null

- **Definition**: The null value in JSON represents an empty or nonexistent value.
- **Example**: null

Practical Use and Considerations

- **Flexibility in Types**: The available data types allow JSON to be extremely flexible. Arrays and objects can be nested within each other, allowing for complex data structures.
- **Type Conversion**: When JSON data is parsed in a programming language, the JSON data types are converted into the native data types of that language. For example, JSON objects convert to Python dictionaries, JSON arrays to Python lists, JSON strings to Python strings, and so on.
- **Strict Syntax Rules**: Despite its flexibility, JSON has strict syntax rules particularly with strings and property names which must always be enclosed in double quotes.

Understanding these data types and how they map to those in various programming languages is crucial for developers working with JSON, whether for configuring systems, coding applications, or interfacing with web APIs. JSON's simplicity, combined with its powerful ability to represent complex data structures, makes it a favorite choice for data interchange across the internet.

Nested Structures in JSON

JSON (JavaScript Object Notation) is highly flexible and capable of representing complex hierarchical data by allowing objects and arrays to be nested within each other. This feature is essential for modeling real-world data structures more accurately and efficiently in JSON format.

Basics of Nesting in JSON

Nesting in JSON involves placing an array or object inside another array or object. This capability allows for the representation of detailed and structured information in a clear and organized manner. Here's how JSON handles these nested structures:

Nested Objects

Objects can contain other objects, creating a nested, hierarchical structure. This is particularly useful for representing entities that have sub-properties or grouped data attributes.

Example of Nested Objects:

```
{
  "employee": {
    "name": "John Doe",
    "address": {"street": "123 Elm St",
    "city": "Somewhere",
    "zipCode": "12345"
    },
    "contactDetails": {
      "email": "john.doe@example.com",
      "phone": "555-1234"
    }
  }
}
```

In this example, the employee object contains nested objects for address and contactDetails. Each nested object encapsulates related attributes, maintaining a clear and logical structure.

Nested Arrays

Arrays can also contain other arrays, allowing for lists of lists. This is useful for representing matrix-like data or complex lists.

Example of Nested Arrays:

```
{
  "matrix": [
    [1, 2, 3],
    [4, 5, 6],
    [7, 8, 9]
  ]
}
```

Here, matrix is an array of arrays, effectively representing a 3x3 matrix.

Objects in Arrays

Arrays can hold objects, providing a way to list multiple entities that each have detailed information.

Example of Objects in Arrays:

```
{
  "employees": [
    {
      "name": "John Doe",
      "department": "HR"
    },
    {
      "name": "Jane Smith",
      "department": "IT"
    }
  ]
}
```

This structure is very common for returning sets of records from an API, where each item in the array represents an employee with properties defined in an object.

Arrays in Objects

Conversely, objects can contain arrays, which is useful for properties that have multiple values.

Example of Arrays in Objects:

```
{
  "employee": {
    "name": "John Doe",
    "skills": ["management", "communication", "analysis"]
  }
}
```

In this example, the skills property is an array containing multiple values, indicating the various skills associated with an employee.

Practical Implications and Considerations

The ability to nest structures in JSON allows for:

- **Modularity**: Elements can be structured in a modular fashion, making the data easier to manage and understand.
- **Scalability**: Data can be added or adjusted easily, such as adding more properties or details to an object without disrupting the overall structure.
- **Flexibility**: Different types of data and their relationships can be accurately represented, reflecting the complexity of real-world data interactions.

Understanding and effectively utilizing nested JSON structures are crucial for developers to efficiently handle multifaceted data, providing a powerful tool for web development, configuration management, and data exchange across diverse systems.

Parsing and Generating JSON in Python

Using the json Module in Python

Python's built-in json module provides a straightforward way to encode and decode JSON data, commonly known as parsing and serialization. This module adheres to the JSON format specifications and is an essential tool for working with JSON data in Python applications.

Importing the json Module

To begin working with JSON data in Python, you first need to import the json module. You can do this with a simple import statement at the beginning of your Python script:

```
import json
```

Primary Functions of the json Module

The json module offers a set of functions that are primarily used for parsing JSON from strings or files (decoding) and for generating JSON strings or writing JSON to files (encoding). Here are the key functions provided by the module:

json.loads()

Purpose: Parses a JSON formatted string and converts it into a Python object.

Usage Example:

```
json_string = '{"name": "John", "age": 30, "city": "New York"}'
data = json.loads(json_string)
print(data['name']) # Output: John
```

json.dumps()

Purpose: Takes a Python object and converts it (serializes it) to a string in JSON format.

Usage Example:

```
data = {
  "name": "John",
  "age": 30,
  "city": "New York"
  }
json_string = json.dumps(data)
print(json_string)
# Output: {"name": "John", "age": 30, "city": "New York"}
```

json.load()

Purpose: Reads JSON data from a file or file-like object and converts it into a Python object.

Usage Example:

```
# Assuming 'data.json' contains the JSON data
with open('data.json', 'r') as file:
  data = json.load(file)
  print(data['name'])
```

json.dump()

Purpose: Takes a Python object and serializes it to a JSON formatted stream to a file or file-like object.

Usage Example:

```
data = {
  "name": "John",
  "age": 30,
  "city": "New York"
  }
with open('output.json', 'w') as file:
  json.dump(data, file)
```

Additional Features and Options

The json module also supports several optional parameters to customize the serialization and parsing processes, such as:

- indent: This parameter can be used with dump() and dumps() to make the output more readable by formatting it with a specified number of spaces for indentation.
- sort_keys: When set to True, the keys in JSON output will be sorted alphabetically.
- ensure_ascii: When set to False, the output can contain non-ASCII characters, which might be useful when working with non-English data.

Python's json module is an efficient and reliable way to work with JSON data, offering powerful tools for converting between JSON and Python data structures. Its simplicity and the broad support of Python data types make it an invaluable resource for developers dealing with JSON in modern web applications, data processing, and IoT implementations.

Reading JSON (Parsing) in Python

Parsing JSON in Python involves converting JSON formatted strings or files into Python objects using the json module. This process is crucial for accessing and manipulating the data in a more familiar Pythonic way. Here are two primary methods for parsing JSON data:

Parsing JSON from a String

When you have JSON data in a string format, you can convert it to a Python dictionary using the json.loads() function. This is particularly useful when receiving JSON data from APIs or storing it in text formats.

Example:

Suppose you receive a JSON string that represents a person's information. Here's how you can parse it:

```
import json

# Example JSON string
json_string = '{"name": "Alice", "age": 25, "city": "New York"}'

# Parsing the JSON string
person = json.loads(json_string)

# Accessing the data
print(person['name']) # Output: Alice
print(person['age']) # Output: 25
print(person['city']) # Output: New York
```

In this example, json.loads() converts the JSON string into a Python dictionary, allowing you to access values using the appropriate keys.

Parsing JSON from a File

Often, JSON data is stored in files, and you can read and parse these files directly using the json.load() function. This approach is used for reading configuration files, large data sets, or data exported from other applications.

Example:

Assume you have a file named person.json that contains the following JSON data:

```
{
  "name": "Alice",
  "age": 25,
  "city": "New York"
}
```

Here's how you can read and parse this file in Python:

```python
import json

# Opening and reading the JSON file
with open('person.json', 'r') as file:
    person = json.load(file)

# Accessing the data
print(person['name']) # Output: Alice
print(person['age']) # Output: 25
print(person['city']) # Output: New York
```

In this case, json.load() reads the file person.json and converts its content into a Python dictionary. The with open(...) syntax ensures that the file is properly opened and closed after reading, which is efficient and important for handling resources correctly.

Practical Tips

- **Error Handling**: When parsing JSON data, it's good practice to handle potential exceptions that may arise, such as json.JSONDecodeError, which occurs if the JSON data is malformed.
- **Encoding**: Ensure that your JSON data is encoded in UTF-8, especially

when dealing with non-ASCII characters.

By understanding these parsing techniques, you can efficiently integrate JSON data handling into your Python applications, enabling you to leverage this popular data format effectively across various programming tasks.

Writing JSON (Generating) in Python

Generating JSON in Python involves converting Python objects into JSON-formatted strings or writing them directly to files. This is commonly required when you need to send data to a web service, save configurations, or log data in a structured format. The json module provides two methods, json.dumps() and json.dump(), to handle these tasks.

Using json.dumps()

The json.dumps() function converts a Python object into a JSON-formatted string. This is useful when you need to serialize your data to send over a network or store it in a text format.

Example:

Suppose you have a Python dictionary with some data about a person, and you want to convert it into a JSON string.

```
import json

# Python dictionary
person = {
  "name": "Bob",
  "age": 30,
  "city": "Chicago",
  "hasPets": False,
  "childrenNames": ["Alice", "John"]
}

# Converting the dictionary to a JSON
string json_string = json.dumps(person, indent=4)

# Output the JSON stringprint(json_string)
```

In this example, json.dumps() is used to serialize the person dictionary. The indent parameter is optional and specifies the number of spaces to use for pretty printing, making the output more readable.

Using json.dump()

The json.dump() function is used to serialize a Python object and write it directly to a file in JSON format. This is particularly useful for saving configurations or data that needs to be persistent between sessions.

Example:

Now let's take the same dictionary and write it to a file named person.json.

```
import json

# Python dictionary

person = {
  "name": "Bob",
  "age": 30,
  "city": "Chicago",
  "hasPets": False,
  "childrenNames": ["Alice", "John"]
}

# Writing the dictionary to a file
 with open('person.json', 'w') as file:
  json.dump(person, file, indent=4)
```

In this case, json.dump() takes the Python dictionary and writes it directly to person.json. Using with open(...) ensures that the file is properly handled without needing to explicitly close it. The indent parameter is again used here for pretty printing.

Practical Considerations

- **Ensure ASCII**: By default, json.dumps() and json.dump() ensure that the output is ASCII-encoded. If you want to keep any Unicode characters as they are, you can set the ensure_ascii parameter to False.
- **Sorting Keys**: You can sort the keys in the JSON output alphabetically by setting the sort_keys parameter to True, which can be useful for creating consistent outputs for version control or comparative purposes.

By understanding how to use json.dumps() and json.dump(), you can efficiently handle JSON data generation in your Python applications, ensuring your data is formatted correctly for easy storage, transmission, and future processing.

Handling Python and JSON Data Types

When working with JSON in Python, understanding the mapping between Python and JSON data types is crucial for effective data interchange. This understanding helps in correctly serializing and deserializing data without data integrity issues. Here's a guide on how these data types correspond and the potential pitfalls you might encounter.

Mapping Python Data Types to JSON

Dictionaries to Objects:

In Python, dictionaries are converted to JSON objects. Keys must be strings in JSON; hence, Python dictionary keys are coerced to strings during the JSON encoding process.

- **Pitfall:** Non-string keys in Python dictionaries can cause issues during serialization. Ensure all keys are strings before serialization.

Lists and Tuples to Arrays:

Python lists and tuples map to JSON arrays.

- **Pitfall**: Tuples are converted to arrays just like lists, so information about the immutability of tuples is lost.

Strings to Strings:

Python string data types are directly mapped to JSON strings.

- **Pitfall**: Ensure that strings in Python are properly encoded (e.g., UTF-

8) to avoid issues during the JSON encoding process, especially with non-ASCII characters.

Integers and Floats to Numbers:

Python's integers and floats are converted to JSON numbers.

- **Pitfall**: JSON does not differentiate between integers and floats. Also, very large integers may lose precision in some environments.

True/False to true/false:

Python's True and False boolean values are converted to their JSON counterparts: true and false.

- **Pitfall**: Direct mapping, no significant pitfalls unless logical errors in usage.

None to null:

Python's None type maps to JSON's null.

- **Pitfall**: Ensure that the usage of None in Python is intentional for data representation as null in JSON.

Handling Special Data Types

Dates and Times:

JSON does not have a specific format for dates and times.

Handling:

Convert Python datetime objects to strings (e.g., ISO format) before serialization. During deserialization, parse these strings back into datetime objects.

- **Pitfall**: Automatic conversion is not available, so manual intervention is necessary.

Decimal Data:

Python's decimal.Decimal, used for precise decimal representation, is not natively supported in JSON.

Handling:

Convert Decimal instances to strings before serialization to preserve precision.

- **Pitfall**: Directly serializing as numbers can lead to loss of precision.

Best Practices

- **Explicit Type Conversion**: When working with data that may not directly map between Python and JSON, explicitly convert data types to the closest equivalent JSON-supported type.
- **Validation and Schema Checking**: Use JSON schema validation tools to ensure that the data structure conforms to expected formats, especially when dealing with complex data.
- **Error Handling**: Implement robust error handling around JSON serialization and deserialization to catch and manage type errors or value errors.

By understanding and appropriately handling the mapping between Python and JSON data types, developers can avoid common pitfalls and ensure smooth data interchange between systems. This not only maintains data integrity but also enhances the reliability of applications that rely on JSON for data exchange.

Practical Examples of JSON in Use

1. Configuration Files

JSON is frequently used for configuration files in software applications due to its readability and simplicity.

Example:

Here's how you might use JSON to store configuration settings for a simple application:

```
{
  "server": "localhost",
  "port": 8080,
  "use_ssl": true,
  "logging_level": "debug"
}
```

Reading and Writing JSON Configuration in Python:

```
import json

# Writing JSON configuration to a file
config = {
  "server": "localhost",
  "port": 8080,
  "use_ssl": True,
  "logging_level": "debug"
}
with open('config.json', 'w') as json_file:
  json.dump(config, json_file, indent=4)

# Reading JSON configuration from a file
with open('config.json', 'r') as json_file:
  config = json.load(json_file)
  print(config)
```

API Interaction

JSON is the de facto standard for data interchange in web APIs.

Example:

Here's how you might interact with a web API that returns JSON data using Python:

```
import requests

# Making a GET request to an API
response = requests.get('https://api.example.com/data')
# Parsing the JSON response
data = response.json()
print(data)
```

This code retrieves data from a hypothetical API and uses the .json() method provided by the requests library to parse the JSON response.

Data Storage and Retrieval

JSON serves as a lightweight format for storing data, especially useful in applications where quick retrieval and simple data manipulation are needed.

Example:

Storing user data in a JSON file and retrieving specific information:

```
users = {
  "users": [
   {"id": 1, "name": "Alice", "email": "alice@example.com"},
   {"id": 2, "name": "Bob", "email": "bob@example.com"}
   ]
 }

# Saving users to a JSON file
with open('users.json', 'w') as file:
  json.dump(users, file, indent=4)

# Retrieving data
with open('users.json', 'r') as file:
  users_loaded = json.load(file)
   for user in users_loaded['users']:
     print(user['name'], user['email'])
```

IoT and Device Communication

In IoT systems, JSON is widely used for sending configuration data and commands between devices and servers, often integrated with MQTT for messaging.

Example:

Sending configuration data to an IoT device using MQTT and JSON:

```
import paho.mqtt.client as mqtt
import json

# Create a MQTT client and connect to the broker
client = mqtt.Client()
client.connect("mqtt.example.com", 1883, 60)

# JSON data to be sent
config = {
  "device_id": 101,
  "interval": 5,
  "sensors": ["temperature", "humidity"]}
config_json = json.dumps(config)

# Publishing the config data to the device's config topic
client.publish("devices/101/config", config_json)
```

In this example, a JSON string containing configuration settings for an IoT device is published to a topic that the device subscribes to, enabling dynamic configuration updates over MQTT.

These examples illustrate the flexibility and utility of JSON across various applications, making it an indispensable tool in modern software development, especially in configurations, APIs, data storage, and IoT communications.

3

Chapter 3: MQTT

What is MQTT and Why Use It?

MQTT (Message Queuing Telemetry Transport) is a lightweight messaging protocol specifically designed to cater to the needs of low-bandwidth, high-latency, or unreliable networks. Ideal for connecting remote devices with a minimal code footprint, MQTT operates on a publish-subscribe model, making it highly efficient for Internet of Things (IoT) applications, where network resources are often limited. Its lightweight nature allows for effective data communication even in environments where network connectivity is intermittent or constrained, providing reliable message delivery across diverse and challenging communication channels.

Advantages of MQTT

MQTT (Message Queuing Telemetry Transport) offers several key advantages that make it an ideal choice for many applications, particularly those involving IoT and remote communication scenarios. Here are the primary benefits of using MQTT:

Low Power Usage:

MQTT is designed to minimize power consumption, making it suitable for battery-operated or power-sensitive devices in IoT ecosystems. Its efficient protocol ensures that devices can remain in sleep mode longer, conserving energy.

Minimal Data Packets:

The protocol is tailored to send and receive small data packets, which reduces bandwidth usage. This is crucial for environments with limited network capacity or where data transmission costs are a concern.

Efficient Distribution to Multiple Receivers:

MQTT uses a publish-subscribe model, which efficiently manages the distribution of messages to multiple clients who are subscribed to particular topics. This model avoids the need for direct and repetitive connections between each sender and receiver, optimizing resource usage.

Reliable Message Delivery:

- MQTT supports multiple levels of Quality of Service (QoS) to accommodate different needs regarding message delivery guarantees:
- QoS 0: Delivers messages at most once without confirmation.
- QoS 1: Ensures messages are delivered at least once by requiring acknowledgments from the receiver.
- QoS 2: Guarantees that messages are delivered exactly once by using a four-step handshake.

Lightweight Protocol:

The MQTT protocol has a small code footprint and requires minimal network bandwidth. This makes it particularly effective for connecting thousands of small devices over the internet.

Last Will and Testament (LWT):

MQTT allows clients to specify a "last will" message that is sent out to the specified recipients if a device unexpectedly loses connection. This feature is vital for monitoring device disconnections and triggering alerts or corrective actions.

Highly Scalable:

Due to its lightweight nature and efficient message distribution model, MQTT scales well from small home networks to large industrial applications involving thousands or even millions of devices.

Secure Communication:

MQTT supports secure communication by integrating with transport layer security mechanisms like TLS/SSL. This ensures that data transmitted over networks is encrypted and secure from unauthorized access.

Retained Messages:

MQTT brokers can retain messages on topics for new subscribers. This means a new subscriber immediately receives the last retained message on the topic, ensuring devices can quickly come up to speed with the latest configurations or important data.

MQTT (Message Queuing Telemetry Transport) is highly versatile and is well-suited for a variety of scenarios, particularly those requiring reliable and efficient messaging under constrained conditions. Here are some typical use cases where MQTT excels:

Internet of Things (IoT) Applications

- **Smart Home Devices**: MQTT is extensively used in smart home ecosystems to control lights, thermostats, security systems, and other home appliances efficiently. Its low bandwidth usage and minimal power consumption make it ideal for communicating between a central hub and various devices around the home.
- **Wearable Technology**: For devices like fitness trackers and smartwatches, MQTT facilitates the efficient transmission of health metrics (e.g., heart rate, steps) to smartphones or directly to the cloud for analysis.

Industrial IoT (IIoT)

- **Manufacturing Automation**: MQTT is used to connect various sensors and actuators on the production floor, enabling real-time monitoring and control of manufacturing processes. This helps in predictive maintenance, optimized energy management, and improved operational efficiency.
- **Supply Chain and Logistics**: In logistics, MQTT allows for real-time tracking of goods and vehicles, providing updates on location, condition, and delivery status, thereby enhancing the efficiency of supply chains.

Real-Time Analytics

- **Financial Services**: In stock trading platforms, MQTT can deliver real-time market data to traders and financial analysts, enabling swift decision-making that can capitalize on momentary market opportunities.

- **Sports and Events**: Real-time data streaming of sports statistics to various stakeholders, including media, coaches, and betting agencies, allowing for immediate insights and actions.

Remote Monitoring and Control

- **Energy Management**: MQTT is used for monitoring and controlling remote energy assets like wind turbines and solar panels. It enables operators to receive real-time data on energy production, equipment health, and environmental conditions.
- **Healthcare**: Remote monitoring of patient vitals using MQTT can alert healthcare providers to changes in a patient's condition in real-time, potentially saving lives in critical care situations.

Vehicle Telematics and Fleet Management

- **Real-Time Vehicle Tracking**: MQTT facilitates the transmission of GPS location and vehicle diagnostics from fleet vehicles back to a central server, enabling efficient route planning and fleet optimization.
- **Autonomous Vehicles**: In autonomous driving systems, MQTT can be used for the real-time exchange of sensor data and control commands between vehicles and control stations.

Consumer Applications

- **Messaging Apps**: Some messaging apps utilize MQTT for instant message delivery, especially in environments where network speed and bandwidth may be limited.

Agricultural Technology

- **Smart Farming**: MQTT is used to connect sensors and devices on farms to help monitor soil moisture levels, weather conditions, and crop health, thereby enabling precise irrigation and farming practices.

These use cases demonstrate the broad applicability of MQTT across different sectors, leveraging its strengths to improve connectivity, efficiency, and responsiveness in a world increasingly driven by real-time data and automation.

Core Concepts of MQTT

Broker: The Heart of MQTT Communication

In the MQTT (Message Queuing Telemetry Transport) protocol, the broker plays a pivotal role in the communication model. It serves as the central server that all MQTT clients connect to and is crucial for managing message distribution and maintaining session state. Here's an in-depth look at the role and responsibilities of an MQTT broker:

Role of the MQTT Broker

The MQTT broker is essentially a server that mediates the interactions between MQTT clients. It receives all messages from the clients, filters them based on the topic, and then distributes these messages to the subscribed clients. This publish-subscribe mechanism ensures that messages are only sent to interested parties (subscribers), rather than broadcasting to all clients.

Managing Connections

- **Client Connections**: The broker handles all incoming connections from clients. It must manage multiple connections simultaneously, maintaining a stable and efficient network communication.
- **Session Management**: For each client, the broker maintains a session, which includes the client's state, subscribed topics, and any undelivered messages (depending on the Quality of Service, QoS, level agreed upon). This session management is crucial for supporting features like persistent connections and clean sessions.

Handling Subscriptions

- **Subscribe/Unsubscribe Requests**: The broker processes all subscribe and unsubscribe requests from clients. This involves updating its internal data structures to accurately reflect the current subscriptions for each topic.
- **Topic Filtering**: The broker uses topic filters to determine which clients have subscribed to the topics for incoming messages. This ensures that messages are correctly routed based on the topic hierarchy and wildcards if used.

Message Dissemination

- **Message Routing**: Once a message is received on a particular topic, the broker determines which clients are subscribed to that topic and forwards the message accordingly. This routing is influenced by the QoS level specified by the publishing client.
- **QoS Management**: The broker ensures that messages are delivered according to the QoS levels:
- **QoS 0 (At most once)**: The broker delivers messages with no confirmation required, providing minimal overhead but no guarantee of delivery.
- **QoS 1 (At least once)**: The broker guarantees that messages are delivered

at least once but may result in duplicate messages. It requires acknowl-edgments from the receiving clients and might need to resend messages if acknowledgments are not received.

· **QoS 2 (Exactly once)**: This is the most reliable but also the most resource-intensive level of service. The broker implements a four-step handshake to ensure that each message is received only once by the intended client.

· **Retained Messages**: The broker has the capability to store the last message sent to a topic as a "retained message." Any client that subscribes to that topic receives the retained message immediately upon subscription, which is crucial for new clients that need the latest state or configuration data.

Security Handling

· **Authentication and Authorization**: The broker is responsible for au-thenticating clients based on credentials provided and authorizing them to publish or subscribe to specific topics, ensuring that clients can only access topics they are permitted to interact with.

Error Handling and Logging

· **Monitoring and Diagnostics**: The broker logs errors and monitors transactions for diagnostic purposes. This helps in maintaining the reliability of the MQTT system and in troubleshooting issues that may arise.

By effectively managing these responsibilities, the MQTT broker enables robust, efficient, and secure message exchange across various devices and applications, making it a cornerstone of any MQTT-based communication system.

Clients in MQTT

In the MQTT (Message Queuing Telemetry Transport) architecture, a client refers to any device that connects to the MQTT broker to send or receive messages. Clients can be anything from small IoT devices, such as sensors and actuators, to large systems like servers or complex applications. These clients play a crucial role in the publish-subscribe model of MQTT, engaging in either publishing or subscribing to messages, or often both.

Definition of an MQTT Client

An MQTT client is any device or application that:

- **Connects to an MQTT Broker**: Clients use the TCP/IP protocol to establish a connection with the broker. Once connected, they can start the message exchange.
- **Sends or Receives Messages**: Depending on their roles, they either publish information to the broker or subscribe to receive information from the broker.
- **Operates under Client-Broker Architecture**: In MQTT, all clients connect to a broker and not directly to each other. The broker is responsible for dispatching all messages between the sending and receiving clients.

Types of MQTT Clients

Publisher (Publishing Clients)

- **Role**: Publishers are clients that send data to the broker. The data is associated with a specific topic, which is like a channel or label that the broker uses to filter and distribute messages to subscribers.
- **Function**: Publishers can be devices like sensors transmitting telemetry data, applications sending alerts, or any system needing to distribute

information.

- **Interaction with Broker**: When publishers send a message, they connect to the broker, specify the topic, and transmit the message. The broker then takes responsibility for the message's delivery to the appropriate subscribers.

Subscriber (Subscribing Clients)

- **Role**: Subscribers are clients that receive data from the broker. They indicate their interest in one or more topics by subscribing to them through the broker.
- **Function**: Subscribers can be applications that need to receive updates or commands, such as a dashboard displaying real-time data or actuators waiting for operational commands.
- **Interaction with Broker**: Subscribers maintain a connection with the broker to receive messages. They subscribe to topics and receive messages whenever new data is published under these topics. Depending on the Quality of Service (QoS) agreed upon, subscribers might send acknowledgments back to the broker for received messages.

Interaction Between Publishers and Subscribers

- **Indirect Communication**: Publishers and subscribers do not communicate directly. Instead, they rely on the broker as an intermediary that manages all message routings.
- **Decoupling**: One of the significant advantages of MQTT is that publishers and subscribers are decoupled. They do not need to know each other's identity, network address, or even be connected at the same time. This decoupling allows for flexible communication scenarios and robust message handling.
- **Quality of Service (QoS)**: Both publishers and subscribers specify the level of QoS they require, which dictates how the broker handles message delivery. This ensures that the needs of different applications can be

met, from minimal overhead delivery to guaranteed and single-time delivery.

By understanding the roles and operations of MQTT clients, developers can better design systems that efficiently use MQTT for reliable and scalable communications in a wide array of applications from IoT to complex distributed systems.

Topics in MQTT

In MQTT, topics are a fundamental component used to categorize and filter messages for distribution among clients. Topics play a crucial role in the MQTT publish-subscribe model, allowing messages to be delivered efficiently to interested subscribers based on the topic of the message.

Role of Topics

- **Logical Organization**: Topics provide a way to logically organize messages into categories. This categorization is essential in scenarios where multiple devices or services communicate different types of information on the same network.
- **Message Filtering**: The MQTT broker uses topics to filter messages and determine which subscribers should receive which messages. Each message published to the broker has an associated topic, and subscribers receive messages based on the topics they have subscribed to.

Topic Hierarchy and Structure

Topics in MQTT are structured hierarchically, much like a filesystem path, using a forward slash (/) as a delimiter. This hierarchical structure allows for organized and scalable topic management.

Example Topic Structure:

- home/livingroom/temperature
- factory/machine1/status
- vehicles/001/gps/location

Each level in the hierarchy represents a different degree of specificity, enabling precise control over the subscription and publication process.

Wildcards in Topic Subscriptions

To enhance flexibility and ease of subscription, MQTT supports the use of wildcards in topic subscriptions. Wildcards allow subscribers to receive messages from multiple topics that match a specified pattern. There are two types of wildcards in MQTT:

Single Level Wildcard (+):

- The + wildcard represents a single level within the topic hierarchy and can be used in place of one topic level.
- **Example**: A subscription to home/+/temperature would receive messages published to home/livingroom/temperature, home/kitchen/temperature, etc., but not home/livingroom/humidity.

Multi-level Wildcard (#):

- The # wildcard represents all levels below a certain point in the topic hierarchy and must always appear at the end of the topic string.
- **Example**: A subscription to home/# would receive every message published to topics starting with home, such as home/livingroom/temperature, home/kitchen/humidity, and home/garage/door/status.

Practical Considerations

- **Topic Design**: Effective topic design is crucial for efficient data transmission. It should reflect the logical structure of the information and devices within the system.
- **Security Considerations**: Be mindful of how topics are used and who has access to subscribe or publish to them, as poorly managed topics can lead to security risks, such as unauthorized access to sensitive data.
- **Performance Impact**: While wildcards offer flexibility, excessive use, especially of multi-level wildcards, can impact the performance of the MQTT broker due to the increased complexity in message routing.

Topics are a powerful feature of MQTT, allowing for detailed and flexible message distribution based on subscriber interest. Proper understanding and management of topics and wildcards are essential for optimizing MQTT communications and ensuring system scalability and security.

Structure of MQTT Messages

MQTT messages are designed to be lightweight to support efficient transmission over networks where bandwidth may be limited. Each message in MQTT consists of two main parts: the header and the payload.

Header

The header in an MQTT message is mandatory and contains critical information about the message. Here are the key components of the header:

- **Fixed Header**: This part of the header is always present and includes the message type (such as CONNECT, PUBLISH, SUBSCRIBE), flags specific to the message type, and the remaining length of the message.
- **Variable Header**: This component of the header may or may not be present depending on the message type. For example, in a PUBLISH

message, the variable header contains the topic name and, if the QoS level is 1 or 2, a message identifier.

- **Dup Flag**: Part of the fixed header, it indicates whether the message is a duplicate of a previously sent message.
- **Retain Flag**: Also in the fixed header, it specifies whether the message should be retained by the broker for new subscribers to the topic.

Payload

The payload of an MQTT message carries the actual data being transmitted. Its presence and size depend on the type of message:

- **PUBLISH Messages**: Contain payloads that hold the application message. This payload can include anything from a simple sensor reading to a complex encoded data structure.
- **Other Messages**: Messages like CONNECT, SUBSCRIBE, or ACKs usually do not have a payload.

Quality of Service (QoS)

Quality of Service (QoS) is a key feature of MQTT that defines the guarantee of delivery for a specific message. There are three levels of QoS, each providing different delivery guarantees:

- **QoS 0 (At most once)**: This is the lowest level of service, where messages are delivered according to the best efforts of the operating environment. Delivery is not guaranteed, and no acknowledgement is sent or expected. This level is used when an application can tolerate missing messages.
- **QoS 1 (At least once)**: At this level, messages are guaranteed to be delivered at least once to the receiver. The sender stores the message until it receives an acknowledgement from the receiver. If no acknowledgement is received within a certain timeframe, the sender will attempt to deliver the message again. This can result in duplicate messages, so the receiver

needs to be prepared to handle potential duplicates.

- **QoS 2 (Exactly once)**: This is the highest quality of service, where messages are guaranteed to be delivered exactly once. This involves a four-way handshake between the sender and receiver to ensure that each message is received only once. This level is used when neither message loss nor duplication can be tolerated, though it incurs the highest overhead.

Each QoS level affects the performance and network traffic differently. Higher levels of QoS ensure better delivery guarantees but at the cost of higher bandwidth consumption and longer delivery times. When designing an MQTT application, choosing the right QoS level is crucial depending on the criticality of the data and the network conditions.

Comparison of MQTT with Other Protocols

MQTT vs. HTTP

MQTT:

- **Connection Type**: MQTT is designed around a persistent, long-lived connection that facilitates continuous communication and quick message delivery.
- **Protocol Overhead**: Very low overhead, as MQTT headers are minimal, especially beneficial in low-bandwidth environments.
- **Data Flow**: MQTT supports bidirectional communication with its publish-subscribe model, which is inherently designed for event-driven scenarios where data must be pushed to multiple receivers efficiently.

HTTP:

- **Connection Type**: HTTP is typically stateless, with each request from a client to a server needing to re-establish connections, which can introduce latency.
- **Protocol Overhead**: Generally higher overhead due to HTTP headers and the need for opening and closing connections repeatedly.
- **Data Flow**: HTTP is unidirectional, where the client initiates requests and the server responds, making it less efficient for real-time data updates unless combined with technologies like WebSockets.

Use Cases:

- **MQTT** is more suitable for IoT and real-time applications where devices frequently exchange messages and require constant connectivity with minimal power consumption.
- **HTTP** is ideal for request-response interactions commonly found in web applications, where the overhead associated with setting up a connection is negligible relative to the size of the data being transferred.

MQTT vs. AMQP

AMQP:

- **Features**: AMQP is a feature-rich messaging protocol that supports a variety of messaging patterns and complex routing scenarios. It offers transaction support, message queuing, reliable delivery, and more.
- **Complexity**: Due to its rich feature set, AMQP is more complex and heavier, which might be overkill for simpler or constrained environments but perfect for enterprise-level systems where robust messaging is crucial.

MQTT:

- **Simplicity**: MQTT is simpler and more lightweight, with fewer features compared to AMQP. This makes it easier to implement and maintain, particularly in environments with limited resources.
- **Efficiency**: MQTT's lightweight nature allows it to perform better in constrained environments or in applications that require minimal data overhead and battery usage.

Use Cases:

- **AMQP** is suited for enterprise applications where robustness, security, and customizability are more critical than low overhead or simplicity.
- **MQTT** is better for scenarios where bandwidth, battery life, and ease of deployment are priorities, such as in many IoT contexts.

MQTT vs. CoAP

CoAP:

- **Designed For**: CoAP is specifically designed for very constrained devices and networks, similar to MQTT. It operates over UDP, making it suitable for environments where TCP might be too resource-intensive.
- **Communication Model**: CoAP supports both request-response and observe-notify interactions, allowing devices to subscribe to resource changes, which is somewhat similar to MQTT's publish-subscribe model.

MQTT:

- **TCP-based**: MQTT operates over TCP/IP, which provides reliable communication but at the cost of higher resource use compared to UDP.
- **Scalability in Distribution**: MQTT excels in scenarios requiring mes-

sages to be efficiently distributed to multiple receivers, which is more challenging with CoAP.

Use Cases:

- **CoAP** is excellent for extremely constrained environments where minimizing data traffic and conserving battery life are critical, and where device-to-device communication might be directly managed without the need for a broker.
- **MQTT** is ideal for applications requiring reliable message delivery across a network of devices with slightly less constrained resources, benefiting from its effective multi-client distribution capabilities.

Choosing the Appropriate Protocol

When selecting a communication protocol, consider the following:

- **Reliability Needs**: If message delivery assurance is crucial, opt for protocols like MQTT or AMQP that support multiple levels of QoS.
- **Resource Constraints**: For highly constrained environments (low power, low bandwidth), consider MQTT or CoAP.
- **Functional Requirements**: For complex routing and transactional support, AMQP might be the necessary choice.
- **Deployment Complexity**: Simpler protocols like MQTT are easier to deploy and maintain compared to AMQP.

By aligning the protocol capabilities with application-specific needs, one can ensure efficient, reliable, and appropriate use of resources in any given implementation.

4

Chapter 4: Setting Up MQTT

Installing an MQTT Broker

Choosing the right MQTT broker is critical for the success of any IoT project or any system that relies on real-time messaging. Below is an overview of some popular MQTT brokers and detailed installation instructions for Mosquitto, one of the most widely used open-source MQTT brokers.

Choosing a Broker

Mosquitto

- **Overview**: Eclipse Mosquitto is a lightweight server that implements MQTT protocols 3.1 and 5.0. Known for its simplicity and suitability for small to moderate size applications, it is an excellent choice for both development and production environments.
- **Use Cases**: Ideal for personal projects, IoT applications, and in cases where a straightforward, easy-to-set-up broker is required.

HiveMQ

- **Overview**: HiveMQ is a MQTT broker designed for enterprise solutions, supporting large-scale deployments and providing extensive plugin options for enhanced functionality.
- **Use Cases**: Best suited for enterprise-level applications that require scalability, advanced security features, and high availability.

EMQ X (now EMQX)

- **Overview**: EMQX is designed for high-throughput messaging and large-scale IoT applications. It supports a million concurrent connections and integrates well with other big data solutions.
- **Use Cases**: Appropriate for large-scale IoT deployments such as smart cities or industrial IoT where massive numbers of devices need reliable connectivity.

Installation Process: Mosquitto

Mosquitto on Various Platforms

On Windows:

Download the Installer:

- Visit the Mosquitto official website and download the latest version of Mosquitto for Windows.

Installation:

- Run the downloaded installer. During the installation, select the option to install the Mosquitto broker and client utilities.
- Make sure to check the box that adds Mosquitto to your system PATH.

Starting the Broker:

- Open Command Prompt as administrator.
- Type mosquitto and press Enter. This starts the Mosquitto broker with the default configuration.

Configuring Windows Firewall (if applicable):

- Allow Mosquitto in your firewall settings to enable external connections.

On Linux:

Installing via Package Manager (for Ubuntu/Debian):

- Open a terminal.
- Update your package list: sudo apt-get update
- Install Mosquitto: sudo apt-get install mosquitto mosquitto-clients

Starting the Broker:

- Mosquitto should start automatically. To check if it's running, use: sudo systemctl status mosquitto
- To start Mosquitto manually, use: sudo systemctl start mosquitto

Configuring Mosquitto (optional):

- Edit the configuration file typically located at /etc/mosquitto/-mosquitto.conf
- Restart Mosquitto to apply changes: sudo systemctl restart mosquitto

On macOS:

Installation Using Homebrew:

- Open a terminal.
- If Homebrew is not installed, install it first from https://brew.sh/.
- Install Mosquitto: brew install mosquitto

Starting the Broker:

- To start Mosquitto: brew services start mosquitto

Verification

Verify Installation:

- On any platform, you can verify that Mosquitto is running by using the command mosquitto_sub -t "#" -v to subscribe to all topics, then publishing a test message from another terminal or device.
- Publish a test message: mosquitto_pub -t 'test/topic' -m 'hello world'
- If setup correctly, the subscriber terminal should display the message: 'test/topic hello world'

This setup guide provides a basis for getting started with Mosquitto as an MQTT broker, ensuring that you can begin testing and developing MQTT applications across different operating systems.

Testing the Setup of Mosquitto MQTT Broker

After configuring and starting the Mosquitto MQTT broker, it is essential to test the setup to ensure everything is working as expected. Here's how you can use MQTT client tools like mosquitto_pub and mosquitto_sub for testing, along with some tips for troubleshooting common issues.

Using MQTT Client Tools

Mosquitto_pub and Mosquitto_sub are command-line utilities that allow you to publish messages to a topic and subscribe to topics to receive messages, respectively. These tools are part of the Mosquitto package and are useful for simple tests of the MQTT environment.

Testing Publish/Subscribe Functionality:

- Open two command line terminals.
- In the first terminal, subscribe to a topic:

```
mosquitto_sub -h localhost -t "test/topic"
```

This command subscribes to the topic test/topic on the broker running on localhost.

- In the second terminal, publish a message to the same topic:

```
mosquitto_pub -h localhost -t "test/topic" -m "Hello MQTT"
```

This sends the message "Hello MQTT" to the topic test/topic.

- Check the first terminal where mosquitto_sub is running. You should see the message "Hello MQTT" appear, indicating that the message was successfully published and received by the subscriber.

Testing with Different Quality of Service (QoS) Levels:

- Modify the publish command to test different QoS levels (0, 1, 2):

```
mosquitto_pub -h localhost -t "test/topic" -m "Test QoS 1" -q 1
```

Replace –q 1 with –q 0 or –q 2 to test QoS levels 0 and 2, respectively.

Troubleshooting Common Issues

Connection Issues:

- **Symptom**: Client tools (mosquitto_pub, mosquitto_sub) cannot connect to the broker.
- **Check**: Ensure the Mosquitto broker is running (systemctl status mosquitto on Linux).
- **Network**: Verify that no firewall or network configuration is blocking the MQTT port (default 1883, or 8883 for TLS).

Authentication Failures:

- **Symptom**: Authentication errors when trying to connect to the broker.
- **Check**: Ensure that the username and password are correctly set up in the broker's password file and are being correctly specified in the client commands.

Message Delivery Issues:

- **Symptom**: Messages are not being received by the subscriber.
- **QoS Configuration**: Check if the QoS levels of the publisher and sub-scriber are appropriately set for the desired delivery guarantees.
- **Topic Mismatch**: Ensure that the publisher and subscriber are using exactly the same topic names, including case sensitivity.

Logging and Debugging:

- Enable verbose logging in Mosquitto to get more detailed output about what the broker is doing:

Security Considerations for MQTT

Security is a critical component of any network communication protocol, especially for MQTT, which is widely used in IoT environments. This section discusses the importance of security in MQTT, outlines key security measures, and provides best practices for maintaining a secure MQTT environment.

Importance of Security in MQTT

- **Critical Nature of IoT**: Many IoT devices control critical infrastructure or collect sensitive data. Security breaches can lead to significant risks including data theft, device manipulation, or severe disruptions.
- **Scale and Accessibility**: IoT devices are often deployed in large numbers and in physically accessible or remote locations, making them vulnerable to attacks.
- **Data Sensitivity**: IoT devices may transmit sensitive data, which, if intercepted, could lead to privacy violations and other serious consequences.

Implementing Security Measures

Authentication

- **Purpose**: Authentication ensures that only authorized devices can connect to the MQTT broker.

Steps to Enable Username and Password Authentication in Mosquitto:

- **Create a Password File:** Use the mosquitto_passwd tool to create and manage a password file. This file will store usernames and passwords for clients.

```
mosquitto_passwd -c /etc/mosquitto/passwd username
```

- **Configure the Broker**: Edit the mosquitto.conf file to include the password file.

```
password_file /etc/mosquitto/passwd
allow_anonymous false
```

- **Restart Mosquitto**: Apply the configuration changes by restarting Mosquitto.

```
sudo systemctl restart mosquitto
```

. Encryption with TLS/SSL

- **Purpose**: Encryption ensures that data transmitted between clients and the broker cannot be easily intercepted or tampered with.

Guide to Setting Up TLS/SSL:

- **Obtain SSL Certificates**: You can use self-signed certificates or obtain them from a certificate authority.
- **Configure Mosquitto to Use TLS/SSL**:
- Edit the mosquitto.conf file to include the paths to your certificate files:

```
listener 8883
cafile /etc/mosquitto/certs/ca.crt
certfile /etc/mosquitto/certs/server.crt
keyfile /etc/mosquitto/certs/server.key
```

- **Restart the Broker**: Restart Mosquitto to enable SSL/TLS on the specified port.

```
sudo systemctl restart mosquitto
```

Access Control with ACLs

- **Purpose**: ACLs restrict which topics clients can publish to or subscribe from, adding a layer of control over data flow.

Steps to Implement ACLs:

- **Define ACL Rules**: Create an ACL file that specifies the allowed operations for each user.

```
user alice
topic readwrite sensors/+

user bob
topic readonly sensors/temp
```

Configure Mosquitto to Use the ACL File:

- Add the ACL file to the mosquitto.conf file:

```
acl_file /etc/mosquitto/acl
```

Restart Mosquitto: Apply the ACL settings by restarting the broker.

```
sudo systemctl restart mosquitto
```

Best Practices for Maintaining a Secure MQTT Environment

- **Regular Software Updates**: Keep the MQTT broker and clients up to date with the latest security patches and updates.
- **Secure Default Settings**: Always start with secure default settings (e.g., disabling anonymous access, using strong passwords).
- **Regular Monitoring and Auditing**: Implement logging and monitoring to detect unusual activities or potential security breaches.
- **Network Segmentation**: Use network segmentation to limit the impact of a breach and restrict access to critical network resources.

By implementing these security measures and adhering to best practices, you can significantly enhance the security of your MQTT deployment, ensuring that both data and device operations are protected against common threats.

5

Chapter 5: Python Libraries for MQTT

Introduction to paho-mqtt

Overview of paho-mqtt

paho-mqtt is a client library that implements the MQTT protocol for Python. It is part of the Eclipse Paho project, which provides scalable open-source client implementations of MQTT and MQTT-SN messaging protocols aimed at new, existing, and emerging applications for Machine-to-Machine (M2M) and Internet of Things (IoT).

Role in the MQTT Ecosystem:

- paho-mqtt enables Python applications to connect to an MQTT broker to publish messages, and to subscribe to topics and receive published messages.
- It implements MQTT protocol versions 3.1 and 3.1.1, and recently MQTT 5.0, thus providing compatibility with a wide range of MQTT brokers.

Features of paho-mqtt

- **Support for Multiple MQTT Versions**: paho-mqtt supports MQTT v3.1, v3.1.1, and v5.0, allowing it to interact with a broad array of MQTT brokers and systems.
- **Automatic Reconnect**: Automatically tries to reconnect to the broker if the connection is lost. This is crucial for IoT applications where consistent connectivity is critical.
- **Asynchronous and Synchronous Client APIs**: paho-mqtt provides both asynchronous (non-blocking) and synchronous (blocking) APIs, giving developers the flexibility to choose the one that best fits their application's architecture.
- **SSL/TLS Support**: Offers the ability to connect over secured layers, ensuring that data transmitted between the client and broker is encrypted and secure.
- **WebSocket Support**: Can connect to MQTT brokers over WebSocket, useful for web applications.
- **Quality of Service (QoS)**: Supports multiple levels of message delivery guarantees (QoS 0, QoS 1, and QoS 2).
- **Last Will and Testament (LWT)**: Allows the specification of an "out-of-band" message to be sent by the broker if it detects that the client has disconnected unexpectedly.

Why Use paho-mqtt

- **Comprehensive MQTT Standard Support**: One of the main advantages of using paho-mqtt is its robust support for different versions of the MQTT standard, making it versatile for use in diverse environments and applications.
- **Robustness**: paho-mqtt is well-tested and widely used in commercial and open-source projects, providing a proven platform for developing reliable MQTT-based applications.
- **Flexibility**: With its support for both synchronous and asynchronous

programming models, paho-mqtt offers flexibility in application design, allowing it to be integrated into a variety of Python applications, from simple scripts to complex, multi-threaded applications.

- **Community and Documentation**: Being part of the Eclipse Foundation, paho-mqtt benefits from a strong community and good documentation, which facilitates easier implementation and troubleshooting.
- **Lightweight and Efficient**: It is designed to be lightweight and efficient, suitable for constrained devices such as those used in IoT deployments.

Using paho-mqtt provides Python developers with a powerful tool for integrating MQTT communication into their applications, leveraging its flexibility, robust support, and comprehensive features to create efficient and reliable IoT or M2M solutions.

Installing and Setting Up paho-mqtt

Installing and setting up paho-mqtt in your Python environment is straight-forward. Here's how you can get started, from installation to setting up a simple project.

Installation Process

Using pip: paho-mqtt can be easily installed using pip, Python's package installer. Follow these steps:

- **Install paho-mqtt**: Open your command line interface (CLI) and execute the following command:

```
pip install paho-mqtt
```

This command downloads and installs the paho-mqtt library and its dependencies.

- **Verifying Installation**: To verify that paho-mqtt has been installed correctly, try importing the library in Python:

```
import paho.mqtt.client as mqtt
print("paho-mqtt is installed successfully!")
```

If you do not encounter any errors during the import, paho-mqtt is installed correctly on your system.

Setting Up a Simple Project

Project Structure: For a basic MQTT project using paho-mqtt, consider the following organizational structure:

- **main.py**: This will be your main script where you set up MQTT client connections, publish messages, and handle incoming messages.
- **config.py**: Contains configuration variables such as broker address, port, topic names, etc.
- **publisher.py** and **subscriber.py**: Optional split of functionality for clarity and modularity, where publisher.py handles message publishing and subscriber.py manages subscriptions and message processing.

Initial Configuration:

- **Creating a Basic MQTT Client**: In your main.py, set up the client and connect it to an MQTT broker.

```
import paho.mqtt.client as mqtt

# Callback function to handle connection events
def on_connect(client, userdata, flags, rc):
    print("Connected with result code "+str(rc))
    # Subscribing in on_connect() means that if we lose the
    #connection and reconnect then subs will be renewed.
    client.subscribe("your/topic")

# Callback function to handle incoming messages
def on_message(client, userdata, msg):
    print(msg.topic+" "+str(msg.payload))
```

```
# Setup MQTT Client
client = mqtt.Client()
client.on_connect = on_connect
client.on_message = on_message

# Connect to the MQTT Broker
client.connect("broker_address", 1883, 60)

# Blocking call that processes network traffic, dispatches
#callbacks and handles reconnecting.
# Other loop*() functions are available that give a
# threaded interface and a manual interface.
client.loop_forever()
```

- **Configure the Broker Details**: In your config.py, define the MQTT broker details:

```
MQTT_BROKER = "broker_address"
MQTT_PORT = 1883
MQTT_TOPIC = "your/topic"
```

- **Running the Project**: Run main.py to start the MQTT client. It should connect to the specified MQTT broker and be ready to publish and receive messages.

This basic setup provides a foundation for developing more complex MQTT applications. You can extend the project by adding more sophisticated message handling, integrating with databases, or implementing security measures like SSL/TLS encryption.

Basic Methods and Callbacks in paho-mqtt

Connecting to a Broker

The connect() Method:

Purpose: The connect() method is used to establish a connection between the MQTT client and the broker.

Usage:

```
import paho.mqtt.client as mqtt

client = mqtt.Client()
client.connect("broker_address", 1883, 60)
```

Parameters:

- broker_address: The hostname or IP address of the broker.
- 1883: The network port of the server (default for MQTT).
- 60: The keepalive interval in seconds.

Handling Network Parameters:

- **Host and Port**: As shown above, the host (broker address) and port are specified in the connect() method.

- **Keepalive**: This parameter helps to ensure that the connection remains open even if no data is being sent. The client will ensure that at least some data (like a ping) travels across the network within each keepalive period.
- **Other Parameters**: You can also specify clean_session, which controls the persistence of the session information on the broker, and will, which sets the "Last Will and Testament" (LWT) of the connection for handling unexpected disconnections.

Publishing Messages

The publish() Method:

- **Purpose**: Used to send a message to a specific topic within the MQTT broker.
- **Usage**:

```
(rc, mid) = client.publish(
                    "topic/path",
                    "Hello MQTT",
                    qos=1,
                    retain=False
                    )
```

Parameters:

- topic: The topic to which the message should be sent.
- payload: The actual message to send.
- qos: Quality of Service level.

- retain: If set to True, the message is retained on the broker until it is replaced by a newer message.

Quality of Service and Retained Messages:

- **QoS Levels**:
- 0: The message is delivered at most once, and delivery is not confirmed.
- 1: The message is delivered at least once, with confirmation required.
- 2: The message is delivered exactly once by using a four-step handshake.
- **Retained Messages**: If a message is published with retain=True, it is stored by the broker as the last known good value for that topic. Any client subscribing to that topic will immediately receive the retained message, even if it subscribes much later.

Subscribing to Topics

The subscribe() Method:

- **Purpose**: Used to subscribe to one or more topics.

Usage:

```
client.subscribe("topic/path")
client.subscribe([("topic/path", 0), ("another/topic", 1)])
```

Parameters:

- topic: A single topic or a list of tuples containing topic names and QoS levels.

Handling Subscriptions with Wildcards:

- Wildcards such as + (single-level) and # (multi-level) can be used to subscribe to multiple topics simultaneously. For example:
- sensor/+/temperature subscribes to temperature topics for any device.
- sensor/# subscribes to all topics starting with sensor/.

Using Callbacks

Event Handling:

- Callbacks are used to handle asynchronous events such as a successful connection, message receipt, or a completed subscription.

Implementing Callbacks:

on_connect

```
def on_connect(client, userdata, flags, rc):
    print("Connected with result code "+str(rc))
    client.subscribe("topic/path")
```

on_message

```
def on_message(client, userdata, msg):
    print(msg.topic+" "+msg.payload.decode())
```

on_publish

```
def on_publish(client, userdata, mid):
    print("Message published: " + str(mid))
```

on_subscribe

```
def on_subscribe(client, userdata, mid, granted_qos):
    print("Subscribed: " + str(mid) + " " + str(granted_qos))
```

Error Handling:

Incorporate error handling within callbacks to deal with unexpected dis-connections or communication errors. For example, use the on_disconnect callback to handle reconnection logic.

Using these methods and callbacks, you can effectively manage MQTT operations in paho-mqtt, ensuring robust communication between your application and the MQTT broker.

6

Chapter 6: Creating Your First MQTT Client

Establishing a Connection to the Broker

Introduction to MQTT Connectivity

In the MQTT protocol, the client-broker model is essential. An **MQTT client** is any device or application that makes a network connection to an MQTT broker/server. The **broker** acts as an intermediary, receiving all messages, filtering them, and then distributing them to clients subscribed to relevant topics. Establishing a stable connection between the client and the broker is crucial for ensuring reliable message delivery and effective communication within the MQTT ecosystem.

Using paho-mqtt for Connection

Configuration

Before connecting to an MQTT broker using paho-mqtt, certain configuration details need to be specified:

- **Broker's URI**: The address of the MQTT broker, which can be an IP address or a DNS name.
- **Port Number**: The network port of the MQTT broker. The default ports are 1883 for non-TLS connections and 8883 for TLS-secured connections.
- **Client ID**: A unique identifier for each client connecting to the MQTT broker. If not specified, many brokers will assign a random ID automatically.
- **Clean Session**: A boolean that determines whether the server should store information about the client between disconnects.
- **Username and Password** (if authentication is required): Credentials required if the broker is configured to require authentication.

The connect() Method

The connect() method of paho-mqtt establishes a network connection to the MQTT broker and is configured as follows:

```
import paho.mqtt.client as mqtt

# Create a client instance
client = mqtt.Client(
                 client_id="your_client_id",
                 clean_session=True
            )

# Configure username and password if enabled
client.username_pw_set("username", "password")

# Connect to the broker
client.connect("broker_uri", 1883, 60)
```

- **broker_uri**: The URI of the MQTT broker.
- **1883**: The port number on which the MQTT broker is listening.
- **60**: The keepalive interval in seconds. This is a time period during which if no other data is exchanged, the client will send a PING message to the broker, ensuring that the connection is kept alive.

Connection Callbacks

Implementing connection callbacks allows handling specific events related to the MQTT connection:

- **on_connect**: This callback is triggered when the client receives a CONNACK response from the MQTT broker. It is a good place to handle initial setup, such as subscribing to topics.

```
def on_connect(client, userdata, flags, rc):
  if rc == 0:
    print("Connected successfully.")
    # Subscribe to a topic
    client.subscribe("topic/path")
  else: print("Connection failed with code ", rc)

# Assign the callback function to the client
client.on_connect = on_connect
```

- **rc (Return Code)**: Indicates the outcome of the connection attempt. An rc of 0 means the connection was successful; other values indicate various errors such as incorrect client credentials, an unavailable broker, etc.

Using these configurations and callbacks effectively can help ensure that your MQTT client maintains a stable and reliable connection to the MQTT broker, handling reconnections and errors gracefully. This setup is essential for deploying robust MQTT applications capable of continuous and efficient operations.

Subscribing to Topics

Understanding MQTT Subscriptions

In MQTT, subscriptions allow clients to receive messages from topics of interest. A **topic** in MQTT is a UTF-8 string that the broker uses to filter messages for each connected client.

- **Topic-based Messaging:** When a message is published to a topic, all clients subscribed to that topic receive the message. The broker handles the distribution of messages to these subscribers.

- **Filtering:** Topics are structured hierarchically (similar to a filesystem path), which allows messages to be categorized in a detailed manner. Clients can subscribe to exact topics or use wildcards to subscribe to multiple topics simultaneously.

Implementing Subscriptions in paho-mqtt

The subscribe() Method

Subscribing to topics in paho-mqtt involves using the subscribe() method, which can be configured to subscribe to one or more topics at various levels of Quality of Service (QoS).

- **Single Topic Subscription:**

```python
import paho.mqtt.client as mqtt
def on_connect(client, userdata, flags, rc):
    print("Connected with result code " + str(rc))
    # Subscribe to a topic
    client.subscribe("home/temperature", qos=1)

client = mqtt.Client()
client.on_connect = on_connect
client.connect("broker_address", 1883, 60)
client.loop_forever()
```

- **Multiple Topic Subscription:**

```
subscriptions = [
                ("home/temperature", 1),
                ("home/humidity", 0)
                ]

client.subscribe(subscriptions)
```

Quality of Service (QoS) Levels

The QoS level determines the guarantee of message delivery:

- **QoS 0 (At most once)**: Delivers the message at most once. The message is not stored and not retransmitted by the broker.
- **QoS 1 (At least once)**: Ensures the message is delivered at least once. The broker might deliver the message multiple times in case of network failure.
- **QoS 2 (Exactly once)**: Guarantees that each message is received only once by the counterpart. It is the safest and slowest quality of service level due to the handshake required to manage message delivery.

Choosing the right QoS level depends on the specific needs and constraints of your application. For instance, critical alert messages might require QoS 1 or 2 to ensure delivery, whereas periodic sensor data might be acceptable at QoS 0.

Subscription Callbacks

- **on_subscribe**: This callback is used to handle the result of the subscribe request.

```
def on_subscribe(client, userdata, mid, granted_qos):
    print(
    "Subscribed: " + str(mid) + " with QoS: " + str(granted_qos)
        )
```

- **on_message**: This callback is triggered whenever a message is received on a topic that the client is subscribed to.

```
def on_message(client, userdata, message):
    print(
            "Received message '" +
            str(message.payload.decode("utf-8")) +
            "' on topic '" +
            message.topic +
            "' with QoS " +
            str(message.qos)
        )
```

By setting up these callbacks, you can effectively manage subscriptions and handle incoming messages. This setup allows you to build robust applications that can react in real-time to MQTT messages from various topics. Integrating these elements into your MQTT client enhances its responsiveness and reliability in operational environments.

Publishing Messages in MQTT

The Role of Publishing in MQTT

Publishing in MQTT refers to the process of sending messages from a client to an MQTT broker under a specific topic. The broker then distributes these messages to all clients that are subscribed to that topic. This model allows for the efficient dissemination of information and real-time communication between multiple devices or services within the MQTT ecosystem.

Using paho-mqtt to Publish Messages

The publish() Method

The publish() method in paho-mqtt is used to send messages to the MQTT broker. It involves specifying the topic under which the message should be published, the payload of the message, and the desired Quality of Service (QoS).

- **Basic Usage:**

```
import paho.mqtt.client as mqtt

client = mqtt.Client()
client.connect("broker_address", 1883, 60)

# Publishing a message
client.publish(
            "home/temperature",
            payload="22.5",
            qos=1,
            retain=False
            )
client.loop_forever()
```

- **topic**: The topic name to which the message is published (e.g., "home-/temperature").
- **payload**: The actual data or message to send. It can be a string, byte array, int, or float.
- **qos**: Quality of Service level (0, 1, or 2).
- **retain**: If set to True, the message is retained by the broker and delivered immediately to new subscribers of the topic.

Publishing Callbacks

- **on_publish**: This callback is triggered when a message has been successfully sent to the broker, providing a means to confirm the publish action.

```
def on_publish(client, userdata, mid):
    print(f"Message {mid} has been published.")
client.on_publish = on_publish
```

- **mid**: The message ID of the publish message, which can be used to track the status of messages.

Best Practices for Publishing

When publishing messages in MQTT, it's important to adopt strategies that enhance the effectiveness and reliability of your messaging:

- **Payload Structuring**: Structure your payload efficiently. For JSON data, ensure it is compact and contains only necessary fields. Avoid sending large or complex data structures unless needed.
- **Topic Naming Convention**: Use a logical and hierarchical topic naming convention that makes it easy to manage and understand. For example, "region/device_id/sensor_type" can be a practical approach.
- **Frequency of Messages**: Adjust the frequency of your messages based on the needs of the application. For real-time monitoring, frequent updates may be necessary, whereas for less critical data, a lower frequency might be sufficient.
- **Handling Connection Persistence**: Ensure the connection to the broker is maintained and managed properly. Use the reconnect() method if the client gets disconnected.
- **Use Retained Messages Wisely**: Use the retain flag judiciously, as retaining every message may not be necessary and could lead to outdated information being sent to new subscribers.
- **Security Considerations**: When sending sensitive data, ensure that the connection is encrypted and that authentication mechanisms are in

place.

By following these guidelines and utilizing the publish() method effectively within paho-mqtt, you can ensure that your MQTT client efficiently communicates and interacts within the MQTT network, thereby enhancing the overall performance and reliability of your IoT or messaging applications.

Handling Connection and Communication Events in paho-mqtt

Proper management of connection and communication events is critical in ensuring the reliability and robustness of applications using MQTT. This includes dealing with disconnections, managing subscriptions, and handling publishing errors efficiently.

Comprehensive Event Management

Significance:

- **Continuous Connectivity**: IoT and other real-time applications rely on continuous and reliable connections to transmit critical data.
- **Resilience**: Proper event management ensures that the application remains operational under various network conditions and can recover from interruptions gracefully.
- **Data Integrity**: Ensuring that messages are delivered correctly and timely, maintaining the integrity and relevance of the data being exchanged.

Implementing Robust Callback Functions

Auto-reconnect Mechanism

paho-mqtt provides support for automatically attempting to reconnect to the broker if the connection is lost. This is crucial for maintaining a persistent connection without manual intervention.

- **Setting Up Auto-Reconnect**:

```python
import paho.mqtt.client as mqtt
def on_connect(client, userdata, flags, rc):
    if rc == 0: print("Connected successfully.")
        # Subscribe or resubscribe to topics
        client.subscribe("some/topic")
    else:
        print(f"Failed to connect, return code {rc}")

def on_disconnect(client, userdata, rc):
    if rc != 0:
        print("Unexpected disconnection.")
# Create and configure the client
client = mqtt.Client()
client.on_connect = on_connect
client.on_disconnect = on_disconnect

# Enable the automatic reconnection feature
client.reconnect_delay_set(min_delay=1, max_delay=120)
# Connect to the broker
client.connect("broker_address", 1883, 60)
# Start the loop
client.loop_forever()
```

This setup not only handles the initial connection but also re-establishes the connection if it is unexpectedly lost.

Error Handling

Handling errors efficiently is vital to the robustness of MQTT applications. This includes errors during connection, subscription, and message publishing.

General Error Handling:

- Use try-except blocks around operations that might throw exceptions, such as network operations.
- Log error details and possibly alert administrators if critical errors occur.

Specific Callbacks:

- **on_connect**: Handle different return codes to determine the nature of the connection failure.
- **on_message**: Ensure the payload is valid and handle cases where the data may be corrupted or in an unexpected format.
- **on_subscribe**: Check the result of subscription requests and handle failures to subscribe to essential topics.

Examples of Error Handling:

```
def on_publish(client, userdata, mid):
    print(f"Message {mid} has been published successfully.")

def on_error(client, userdata, mid):
    print(f"Failed to publish message {mid}.")
    # Implement retry logic or log the error for later analysis
```

By adopting these practices for auto-reconnection and error handling, you ensure that your MQTT clients can handle network variations and other issues gracefully. This not only enhances the user experience but also boosts the reliability of the system, ensuring that it remains functional and efficient under different operational conditions.

Testing and Troubleshooting Your MQTT Client

Ensuring that your MQTT client functions correctly and reliably is critical, especially in applications that depend on real-time data transmission. Here are effective methods for testing your MQTT client and troubleshooting common issues.

Testing Your MQTT Client

Use of MQTT Test Servers:

- **Public Brokers**: Utilize public MQTT brokers available for testing purposes, such as test.mosquitto.org or broker.hivemq.com. These brokers allow you to quickly set up and test MQTT functionalities without the need to configure your own broker.

Testing Procedure:

- Connect your MQTT client to a public test broker.
- Subscribe to a topic, for example, test/topic.
- Use another MQTT client to publish messages to the same topic.
- Verify that messages are received by your client.

Local Broker Setup:

- **Dedicated Test Environment**: Set up a local MQTT broker on your development machine or within your local network. Tools like Mosquitto can be easily installed and run on most operating systems.

- **Isolated Testing**: This allows you to test in a controlled environment, which is especially useful for debugging network issues or testing client reconnections and other resilience features.

Automated Testing:

- **Unit Tests**: Write unit tests for your client's logic to ensure that message handling, topic subscription, and publishing work as expected under various scenarios.
- **Integration Tests**: Set up scenarios that mimic real-world operations, including interactions with other systems and the MQTT broker.

Troubleshooting Common Issues

Connectivity Problems:

- **Symptoms**: Client fails to connect to the broker.

Checks:

- Verify the network connection.
- Ensure the broker is running and accessible.
- Check if the correct port is used (default is 1883, or 8883 for TLS).
- Review the client and broker logs for errors.

Resolution:

- Correct any network issues, ensure the broker's address and port configuration are correct, and verify firewall settings are not blocking the connection.

Message Delivery Failures:

- **Symptoms**: Messages are not being published or received as expected.

Checks:

- Confirm that the topic names are correct and match between publisher and subscriber.
- Ensure the Quality of Service (QoS) levels meet the requirements for the use case.
- Check for retained message settings if old data is being received.

Resolution:

- Adjust QoS settings, verify topic names, and check retained settings on the broker.

Subscription Mismatches:

- **Symptoms**: Not receiving messages for subscribed topics.

Checks:

- Ensure the subscription topics correctly match the publishing topics.
- Use wildcards appropriately.
- Check the ACLs (Access Control Lists) if using, to ensure the client has permission to subscribe to the intended topics.

Resolution:

- Correct any discrepancies in topic names, adjust wildcard usage, and modify ACLs as necessary.

Logging and Monitoring:

- Continuously log client and broker activities.
- Use monitoring tools to watch network traffic and message flows to detect anomalies or performance issues.

By systematically applying these testing and troubleshooting strategies, you can ensure your MQTT client operates reliably and efficiently, handling real-world data communication demands effectively. This approach is essential for maintaining high-quality MQTT-based applications.

7

Chapter 7: Integrating JSON with MQTT

Structuring JSON Messages for Efficient Communication

Importance of Message Structure

In MQTT applications, which often involve the transmission of data across networks with limited bandwidth or where devices have constrained resources, the structure of JSON messages is critical. Well-structured JSON ensures:

- **Efficient Data Transmission**: Minimizes network traffic by reducing message size.
- **Ease of Parsing**: Simplifies the process by which devices and servers parse and interpret the data.
- **Scalability**: Properly structured messages are easier to scale with increasing data or more complex application scenarios.
- **Interoperability**: Ensures that different systems or components that use the data can interpret it correctly and consistently.

Designing JSON Schemas

Basic Principles:

1. **Simplicity**: Keep the schema as simple as possible with clear key names that accurately describe their values.
2. **Clarity**: Use consistent and predictable structures that make it easy for developers to understand and use the data correctly.
3. **Necessity**: Include only the data that is necessary for the intended purpose, avoiding any superfluous information that adds to the payload size.

Examples of JSON Structures:

· **Telemetry Data from IoT Devices**:

```
{
    "deviceId": "sensor_001",
    "timestamp": "2024-07-10T14:55:30Z",
    "readings": {
                "temperature": 22.5,
                "humidity": 48
            }
}
```

· **Configuration Updates**:

```
{
   "deviceId": "controller_019",
   "updated": "2024-07-10T15:00:00Z",
   "config": {
           "threshold": {
                           "temperature": 25,
                           "humidity": 50
                           },
               "alertsEnabled": true
           }
}
```

· **Command Messages**:

```
{
   "deviceId": "actuator_045",
   "command": "activate",
   "parameters": {
                   "duration": 120,
                   "intensity": "high"
                   }
}
```

Optimization Techniques

Reducing Payload Size:

· **Minimize Key Names**: Use shorter key names while maintaining clarity. For example, use "temp" instead of "temperature" where context allows.

- **Omit Unnecessary Data**: Do not include data that is not used. For instance, if the device type is always known, there's no need to include it in every message.
- **Use Arrays Effectively**: When sending multiple similar data items, use an array rather than separate objects. For example, sending multiple temperature readings in one array.

Versioning and Compatibility:

- **Schema Versioning**: Include a version number in your JSON messages to handle changes over time. This allows the receiving system to understand how to process the data according to the correct schema.
- **Backward Compatibility**: Design changes to the schema to be backward compatible. For instance, adding new keys is usually safe, but removing keys or changing their meaning requires careful planning and communication with all data consumers.

By adhering to these principles and techniques, you can ensure that your JSON messages are optimally structured for efficient transmission and processing in MQTT applications, supporting effective and scalable communication strategies.

Encoding and Decoding JSON Messages in Python

Using the json Module

Python's json module is a simple and powerful toolkit for encoding and decoding JSON data. Here's how you can use it to convert between Python objects and JSON formatted strings.

Encoding JSON:

- **Purpose**: Convert Python dictionaries or lists into JSON strings.
- **Method**: Use json.dumps().
- **Example**:

```
import json

data = {
        "name": "John Doe",
        "age": 30,
        "is_employee": True,
        "skills": [
                "Python",
                "JavaScript"
                ]
        }

json_string = json.dumps(data, indent=4)
print(json_string)
```

This will output a nicely formatted JSON string with the contents of the Python dictionary.

Decoding JSON:

- **Purpose**: Parse JSON strings back into Python objects (typically dictionaries).
- **Method**: Use json.loads().
- **Example**:

```
import json

json_string = '{
            "name": "John Doe",
            "age": 30,
            "is_employee": true,
            "skills": [
                        "Python",
                        "JavaScript"
                    ]
        }'

data = json.loads(json_string)
print(data)
```

This will convert the JSON string back into a Python dictionary.

Handling Data Types

Not all Python data types can be directly converted to JSON and vice versa. Here's how to handle specific data types:

Dates:

- **Challenge**: JSON does not have a specific format for dates.
- **Solution**: Convert datetime objects to string format before encoding and parse them back into datetime objects after decoding.
- **Example**:

```
from datetime import datetime

import json

# Encoding
current_time = datetime.now()
data = {"timestamp": current_time.isoformat()}
json_data = json.dumps(data)

# Decoding loaded_data = json.loads(json_data)
timestamp = datetime.fromisoformat(
                                    loaded_data[
                                        "timestamp"
                                    ]
                            )
```

Binary Data:

- **Challenge**: JSON does not support binary data.
- **Solution**: Encode binary data in a format such as Base64 before encoding it to JSON.
- **Example**:

```
import base64
import json

# Encoding binary data
bin_data = b'binary\x00data'
bas64_enc_data = base64.b64encode(bin_data).decode('utf-8')
json_data = json.dumps({"file": base64_encoded_data})

# Decoding binary
data loaded_data = json.loads(json_data)
binary_data = base64.b64decode(loaded_data["file"])
```

Efficiency Considerations

Performance Tips:

- **Use Faster Libraries**: While Python's built-in json module is sufficient for many use cases, libraries like ujson or orjson offer significant speed improvements for JSON encoding and decoding.
- **Example**:

```
import ujson

data = {"name": "John", "age": 30}
json_string = ujson.dumps(data)
```

Caching:

- **Purpose**: Reduce the need to repeatedly encode or decode the same data.
- **Method**: Implement caching mechanisms to store pre-encoded JSON strings or pre-decoded Python objects, especially for frequently accessed data.
- **Example**:

```
from functools import lru_cache

@lru_cache(maxsize=32)
def get_json_data(data):
    return json.dumps(data)
```

- **Minimizing Data Size**: As discussed earlier, reducing the payload size by shortening keys and removing unnecessary data can also improve performance by reducing processing overhead.

By effectively managing data types and performance, you can optimize the JSON handling in your Python applications, ensuring efficient and scalable data interchange.

Handling JSON in MQTT Callbacks

Integrating JSON Handling in Callbacks

Handling JSON efficiently in the MQTT callbacks ensures that data transmitted between clients and brokers is processed correctly and efficiently.

Receiving Messages:

- **Purpose**: Decode JSON payloads received in MQTT messages.
- **Implementation in on_message Callback**:

```
import json

import paho.mqtt.client as mqtt
def on_message(client, userdata, message):
    try:
        # Decode the JSON data
        payload = json.loads(message.payload.decode('utf-8'))
        print("Received message:", payload)
        # Process the data
    except json.JSONDecodeError:
        print("Invalid JSON received")

client = mqtt.Client()
client.on_message = on_message
client.connect("broker_address", 1883, 60)
client.subscribe("topic/path")
client.loop_forever()
```

This callback decodes the JSON payload from the received message and processes it. Errors in JSON formatting are caught and handled gracefully.

Sending Messages:

- **Purpose**: Encode data into JSON format before publishing it to an MQTT topic.
- **Guidance**:

```
def publish_json(client, topic, data):
    json_payload = json.dumps(data)
    client.publish(topic, json_payload)
```

Error Handling

Common JSON Errors:

- **Parsing Errors**: Occur when the incoming message does not contain valid JSON, possibly due to data corruption or a sender's mistake.
- **Schema Mismatches**: Happen when the JSON structure doesn't match the expected schema, which can lead to runtime errors if not handled.

Robust Error Handling Strategies:

- **Validating JSON Against a Schema**:
- Use JSON schema validation libraries, such as jsonschema, to validate JSON data against a predefined schema both before sending and after receiving JSON messages.
- **Example**:

```
from jsonschema import validate, ValidationError

schema = {
        "type": "object",
        "properties": {
                "name": {"type": "string"},
                "age": {"type": "integer","minimum": 0}
                },
        "required": ["name", "age"]
        }

def validate_json(data):
  try:
    validate(instance=data, schema=schema)
  except ValidationError as e:
  print("Invalid data:", e)
    return False
  return True
```

Advanced Techniques

Asynchronous Processing:

- **Purpose**: Process JSON data asynchronously to prevent blocking the main thread, especially useful when dealing with large datasets or when maintaining responsiveness is critical.

Implementation:

- Use Python's asyncio module or threading to handle JSON operations in the background.
- **Example**:

```
import asyncio

async def process_data_async(data):
    await asyncio.sleep(0) # Simulate async operation
    print("Processing data:", data)

def on_message(client, userdata, message):
    data = json.loads(message.payload.decode('utf-8'))
    asyncio.run(process_data_async(data))
```

Security Considerations:

Data Integrity and Confidentiality:

- Use MQTT over TLS/SSL to secure the transport of JSON data.
- Consider encrypting sensitive JSON fields before transmission, especially if they contain personal or critical information.

By implementing these techniques and strategies for handling JSON in MQTT callbacks, developers can ensure that their applications not only perform efficiently but also handle data securely and robustly in various scenarios.

8

Chapter 8: Quality of Service (QoS) Levels

Overview of QoS in MQTT

In MQTT (Message Queuing Telemetry Transport), Quality of Service (QoS) is a crucial concept that defines the level of assurance for the delivery of messages between clients and the broker. QoS in MQTT ensures that messages are delivered reliably and efficiently, accommodating various network conditions and application requirements.

Importance of QoS:

- **Reliability**: QoS settings in MQTT provide mechanisms to control how messages are delivered, ensuring that data reaches its destination reliably, which is critical in applications where data must be accurate and up-to-date.
- **Resource Management**: Different QoS levels allow for better management of network and system resources by aligning the level of message delivery assurance with the application's needs.

The Need for Different QoS Levels

MQTT supports three levels of QoS, catering to different requirements of message delivery:

QoS 0 (At Most Once):

- **Description**: The message is delivered at most once, and no confirmation is sent or received. The message may be lost due to network issues but is not re-sent.
- **Use Case**: Best used where an occasional loss of messages is acceptable and does not impact the application significantly. Examples include periodic sensor data updates where only the latest reading is relevant.

QoS 1 (At Least Once):

- **Description**: Ensures that messages are delivered at least once to the receiver. The sender stores the message until it receives an acknowledgment from the receiver. If the acknowledgment is not received, the message is sent again.
- **Use Case**: Suitable for scenarios where message loss cannot be tolerated, but message duplication is acceptable. For instance, control messages in smart home applications, where it is crucial that a command is received, but duplicates do not have adverse effects.

QoS 2 (Exactly Once):

- **Description**: Provides the highest level of assurance by ensuring that each message is received exactly once by the intended recipient. This involves a four-step handshake between the sender and the receiver, making it the most reliable but also the most resource-intensive.
- **Use Case**: Essential for applications requiring both high reliability and exact message counts without duplication, such as financial transactions

or critical command and control systems where each message has significant implications.

Choosing the Right QoS Level:

- The selection of the QoS level should be driven by the application's specific requirements for reliability, network bandwidth, and performance. For example:
- Applications that can tolerate some loss of data might opt for QoS 0 to reduce network traffic and improve performance.
- In contrast, applications that require guaranteed delivery but can handle duplicate messages may find QoS 1 sufficient.
- Applications that cannot afford loss or duplication of messages should use QoS 2, despite its higher resource and performance costs.

Understanding and selecting the appropriate QoS level is fundamental to optimizing MQTT's functionality and ensuring that the application behaves as expected under varying network conditions and operational requirements.

QoS Level 0 - At Most Once

Definition and Use Cases

QoS Level 0, often referred to as "At Most Once," is the simplest and lowest level of Quality of Service in the MQTT protocol. It is sometimes described as a "fire-and-forget" approach because the message is sent only once without any acknowledgment or retransmission mechanism.

- **How It Works**: When a message is published with QoS 0, it is delivered across the network to the intended recipients (subscribers) without any guarantee that it will arrive. There is no feedback mechanism to inform the sender whether the message has been delivered successfully. The broker or client does not retain the message, nor does it attempt to re-deliver it, regardless of whether it reaches the destination or not.

Use Cases:

- **Non-critical Data Updates**: Perfect for scenarios where the data being sent is non-critical and can tolerate some degree of loss, such as periodic updates from sensors where only the most recent reading is relevant (e.g., temperature, humidity readings in a non-critical environment).
- **High-frequency Updates**: Suitable for high-volume or high-frequency data transmissions where not every single data point is crucial, or the next message will quickly supersede the previous one.
- **Bandwidth Conservation**: Ideal in bandwidth-constrained environments where minimizing data traffic is a priority.

Advantages and Disadvantages

Advantages:

- **Low Overhead**: QoS 0 involves the least amount of overhead, both in terms of bandwidth and processing power, as it does not require the broker to store the message or manage any acknowledgments.
- **High Throughput**: Due to its minimal protocol overhead, it allows for higher message throughput compared to higher QoS levels.
- **Simplicity**: The simplest form of message delivery, with no session persistence concerns or elaborate handshake processes.

Disadvantages:

- **No Delivery Guarantee**: The most significant disadvantage of QoS 0 is the lack of any delivery guarantee. Messages may be lost due to network issues, and there is no mechanism to detect or recover from such losses.
- **Unsuitable for Critical Data**: It is not suitable for situations where message delivery is crucial. For instance, command and control messages

that operate machinery or trigger actions in business-critical systems should not use QoS 0.

- **Potential Data Gaps**: In monitoring applications, using QoS 0 can lead to data gaps where lost messages result in missing data points, which could skew analysis or decision-making.

When to Use QoS Level 0:

- Choosing to use QoS level 0 should be driven by the specific needs of the application and the environment in which it operates. It is best used when the application can tolerate occasional message loss, where network efficiency is a priority, and where the potential cost of lost data does not outweigh the benefits of reduced network traffic and higher throughput.

QoS Level 1 - At Least Once

Definition and Use Cases

QoS Level 1, referred to as "At Least Once," ensures that messages are delivered at least once to the receiver but may also result in message duplication in certain scenarios. This level of service strikes a balance between reliability and overhead, making it one of the most commonly used QoS levels in MQTT applications.

- **How It Works**: When a message is published with QoS level 1, the sender stores the message until it receives an acknowledgment (PUBACK) from the receiver. If the sender does not receive an acknowledgment within a reasonable timeframe, it will resend the message, potentially leading to duplicates if the original message was actually received but the acknowledgment was lost.

Use Cases:

- **Command and Control Operations**: Suitable for operations where commands must be received and acted upon, such as turning on lights or starting a machine, where duplicate commands have minimal adverse effects.
- **Ensuring Data Delivery**: Ideal for applications where it's crucial that data is received, such as status updates or alerts in smart home or industrial automation systems.

Message Duplication

Handling Duplications:

- Since QoS level 1 does not guarantee that messages are delivered only once, applications must be designed to handle possible duplications. Here's how MQTT and applications generally deal with this issue:
- **MQTT's Mechanism**: MQTT includes a mechanism for handling message retries. Each message is assigned an identifier (packet identifier), which is used to recognize duplicate messages. However, this does not prevent duplicates from being delivered; it merely identifies them.

Application Handling:

- **Idempotent Operations**: Ensure that operations performed as a result of receiving a message are idempotent—that is, performing them multiple times has the same effect as performing them once. This is particularly important for command messages.
- **Tracking State**: Implement logic in the application to keep track of the state or sequence of received messages. This could involve checking timestamps, sequence numbers, or other unique identifiers included in the message payload.
- **De-duplication Logic**: Develop de-duplication logic within the appli-

cation that can recognize and discard duplicated messages based on message content or a custom identifier.

Advantages and Disadvantages

Advantages:

- **Reliability**: Improved reliability over QoS 0 as messages are guaranteed to be delivered at least once.
- **Moderate Overhead**: Involves more overhead than QoS 0 but significantly less than QoS 2, making it a good middle-ground option.

Disadvantages:

- **Potential for Duplication**: The main drawback is the potential for receiving duplicate messages, which can complicate application logic if not handled correctly.
- **Increased Latency and Bandwidth**: Due to the acknowledgment process, there might be a slight increase in latency and bandwidth usage compared to QoS 0.

QoS Level 2 - Exactly Once

Definition and Use Cases

QoS Level 2, referred to as "Exactly Once," is the highest and most reliable Quality of Service level in MQTT. This QoS ensures that each message is delivered exactly once to the receiver, eliminating any chances of duplication, which is crucial for certain types of applications.

- **How It Works**: The delivery process for QoS level 2 involves a four-step handshake mechanism between the sender and the receiver:
- **PUBLISH**: The sender sends a message with a specific packet identifier.

- **PUBREC (Publish Received)**: The receiver acknowledges the receipt of the message and sends a PUBREC message back.
- **PUBREL (Publish Release)**: Upon receiving PUBREC, the sender sends a PUBREL message to the receiver to initiate the release of the message.
- **PUBCOMP (Publish Complete)**: The receiver sends a PUBCOMP message back to the sender to confirm the message has been processed, completing the exchange.

Use Cases:

- **Financial Transactions**: Ensuring that monetary or transactional data is not duplicated or lost.
- **Critical Command and Control Systems**: In systems where commands must be executed once and only once, such as in medical devices or industrial automation where actions must be precisely controlled.
- **Regulatory and Compliance**: Applications where data integrity and accuracy are required by regulatory standards.

Implementation Challenges

Complexity and Overheads:

- **Resource Intensive**: QoS level 2 is the most resource-intensive among the QoS levels due to the complex handshake mechanism. This process consumes more bandwidth and processing power than QoS 0 and QoS 1.
- **Increased Latency**: The multi-step communication required to ensure message delivery exactly once can lead to higher latency. This may not be suitable for time-sensitive applications.
- **Handling Failures**: The stateful nature of the communication process requires maintaining the state of the message until the transaction is fully complete, which can complicate client and broker implementations, especially in handling failures and ensuring state recovery.
- **Scalability Issues**: The overheads associated with QoS level 2 can become

more pronounced as the system scales up in terms of the number of messages or the number of clients, potentially impacting overall system performance.

Best Practices

Given the complexity and overheads associated with QoS level 2, it is vital to consider whether the need for exact message delivery justifies these costs:

- **Limit Use**: Employ QoS level 2 selectively for those messages that absolutely require it, while using lower QoS levels for less critical messages.
- **Optimize Message Flow**: Design the system to minimize the flow of critical messages that would require QoS level 2, possibly by aggregating data or reducing message frequency.
- **Robust Implementation**: Ensure that the MQTT client and broker implementations are robust and can handle the complexities of QoS level 2 without losing messages, especially in scenarios involving network issues or system failures.

Choosing the Right QoS Level

Selecting the appropriate Quality of Service (QoS) level in MQTT is crucial for ensuring efficient and reliable message delivery that aligns with the specific needs and constraints of your application. Here's how to determine the best QoS level based on various factors and best practices for applying QoS levels in different scenarios.

Factors to Consider

Network Reliability:

- If your network is generally unreliable or experiences frequent disconnections, higher QoS levels (1 or 2) might be necessary to ensure message
delivery.
- For stable and reliable networks, QoS 0 might be sufficient, especially
for non-critical data.

Application Criticality:

- **Critical Applications**: For applications where the accuracy and reliability of every message are crucial (e.g., financial transactions, health
monitoring systems), QoS 2 is often justified despite its overhead.
- **Moderately Critical Applications**: If message delivery must be assured
but occasional duplicates are manageable, QoS 1 provides a good balance.
- **Non-critical Applications**: Where the timeliness or presence of every
single message is not crucial, QoS 0 is adequate and most efficient.

Performance Requirements:

- **Latency Sensitivity**: Applications sensitive to delays (e.g., real-time
control systems) may need to avoid QoS 2 due to its potential latency
implications.
- **Throughput Requirements**: High-throughput systems, where large
volumes of messages are sent, might favor QoS 0 or 1 to avoid the
significant bandwidth and processing overhead associated with QoS
2.

Resource Availability:

- Consider the computational and memory resources of the client and broker systems. Higher QoS levels require more resources for maintaining
message states and handling acknowledgments.

Best Practices

Use QoS Level Appropriately:

- Employ QoS 0 for frequent or regular updates where receiving the latest message is more important than missing a message.
- Use QoS 1 for alerts and notifications where delivery must be guaranteed, but exact duplication is not critical.
- Reserve QoS 2 for critical settings where message duplication or loss cannot be tolerated.

Consistent Application:

- Apply consistent QoS levels across messages of similar importance or type to simplify system behavior and debugging.

Monitoring and Adjustment:

- Regularly monitor the performance and reliability of your MQTT messaging. Adjust QoS levels as needed based on changing network conditions or application requirements.

Testing Different Scenarios:

- Test your MQTT implementation under different network conditions and with various QoS settings to understand their impact and to ensure your system behaves as expected.

Balancing Trade-offs:

- Balance the trade-offs between reliability, performance, and resource usage. For example, while QoS 2 ensures reliability, it may not always be practical if it leads to unacceptable delays or resource drain.

By carefully considering these factors and applying best practices, you can effectively choose the right QoS level for your MQTT applications, ensuring efficient, reliable, and appropriate message delivery tailored to the specific needs of your system.

9

Chapter 9: Retained Messages and Last Will and Testament

Retained Messages in MQTT

Definition of Retained Messages

In MQTT, a **retained message** is a type of message that the broker stores for a specific topic. Unlike regular messages, which are delivered immediately to currently subscribed clients and then discarded, a retained message is saved by the broker and sent to any client that subsequently subscribes to that topic. This ensures that new subscribers immediately receive the most recent state of a topic without having to wait for the next update.

- **How It Works**: When a message is published with the retained flag set to true, the MQTT broker stores that message and replaces any previously retained message on that topic with the new one. This message is then delivered immediately to any future subscribers of that topic, along with any new messages that are published.

Usage Scenarios

Retained messages are particularly useful in scenarios where it's important for clients to get the latest state as soon as they subscribe to a topic:

Status Updates:

- **Example**: A device in a smart home publishes the current state of a light (on or off) as a retained message to the topic home/livingroom/light. Any client that later subscribes to this topic receives the current state of the light immediately upon subscription, ensuring the client is synchronized with the actual state.

System Configurations:

- **Example**: An IoT device can publish its configuration settings (like thresholds or operation modes) as retained messages. This allows any management or diagnostic tool that connects to the system to instantly receive current configurations without needing a request/response cycle.

Sensor Readings:

- **Example**: A weather station publishes the latest weather readings (temperature, humidity, etc.) as retained messages. Any client interested in the current weather conditions gets the latest readings as soon as they subscribe, which is crucial for applications that require immediate data upon startup.

Pros and Cons

Advantages:

- **Immediate Updates for New Subscribers**: New or reconnecting clients receive the most recent message immediately upon subscribing to a topic, which is very effective for displaying the latest state.
- **Reduces Network Traffic**: Avoids the need for new subscribers to request an update, reducing the number of messages flowing through the network.
- **Simplifies Client Logic**: Clients don't need to implement additional logic to check or request the current state; they automatically receive it when they subscribe.

Potential Pitfalls:

- **Stale Data**: If not managed properly, retained messages might become outdated, especially if the device that publishes updates goes offline or stops updating.
- **Security and Privacy**: Retained messages could pose security or privacy risks if sensitive data is retained on a broker, particularly if the broker configuration allows unauthorized subscriptions.
- **Resource Usage**: Storing retained messages consumes additional broker resources (memory and disk), which can become significant depending on the number of topics and the size of the retained messages.

Best Practices:

- Regularly update retained messages to ensure they reflect the current state.
- Implement security measures to control access to topics with retained messages.
- Monitor and manage the impact of retained messages on system resources.

By understanding and leveraging retained messages appropriately, you can significantly enhance the responsiveness and efficiency of MQTT-based applications, ensuring that clients always have access to the most current data relevant to their functions.

Configuring Retained Messages in MQTT

Retained messages in MQTT provide a valuable mechanism for ensuring that new subscribers immediately receive the most current data without having to wait for the next update. Here's how to configure these messages and understand their impact on subscribers.

How to Set a Message as Retained

Setting a message as retained in MQTT involves a simple configuration step during the message publishing process. Here's how you can do this using a typical MQTT client library, such as paho-mqtt in Python:

- **Establish a Connection**: First, ensure your MQTT client is connected to the broker.

```
import paho.mqtt.client as mqtt

client = mqtt.Client()
client.connect('broker_address', 1883, 60)
# Connect to the MQTT broker
```

- **Publish a Retained Message**: When publishing a message, set the retain flag to True. This tells the MQTT broker to hold onto the message and send it to any future subscribers of the topic.

```
topic = 'home/temperature'
payload = '23°C'
qos = 1

client.publish(topic, payload=payload, qos=qos, retain=True)
```

- **topic:** The MQTT topic to which the message is published.
- **payload:** The message content.
- **qos:** Quality of Service level (0, 1, or 2). While QoS is independent of the retain flag, using QoS 1 or 2 with retained messages ensures more reliable delivery.
- **retain=True:** Marks the message as retained.
- **Disconnect**: After publishing the retained message, you may disconnect if no further communication is needed.

```
client.disconnect()
```

Impact on Subscribers

New Subscribers:

- When a new client subscribes to a topic with a retained message, it immediately receives the last retained message published to that topic.

This ensures that the subscriber has the latest relevant data upon subscribing, which is particularly useful for devices that need to initialize with the current state of the system or for users who need immediate updates upon starting an application.

Existing Subscribers:

- For clients that are already subscribed to a topic when a retained message is published, the behavior is just like that of any normal message; the retained message is delivered according to the current subscription's QoS settings.
- However, if these subscribers disconnect and later reconnect, upon re-subscription, they will receive the latest retained message, which might be different from the last message they received before disconnection.

Considerations:

- **Message Freshness**: It's important to ensure that retained messages are updated whenever newer data is available. Stale retained messages can lead to misinformation and errors in operation.
- **Resource Use**: Retained messages are stored in the broker's memory (and possibly on disk, depending on the broker's configuration). Large numbers of retained messages, particularly with large payloads or at high QoS levels, can consume significant resources.
- **Security**: Because retained messages can be delivered to any subscriber of a topic, consider the security implications. Sensitive data should not be sent in retained messages without proper security measures, such as encryption or restricted topic access.

By understanding how to configure and the impacts of retained messages, you can better leverage MQTT's capabilities to enhance real-time data delivery and system initialization processes in IoT and other MQTT-driven environments.

Last Will and Testament (LWT) Feature in MQTT

Purpose of LWT

The **Last Will and Testament (LWT)** feature in MQTT is a mechanism designed to notify other clients about an unexpectedly disconnected client. This feature is crucial for handling cases where a client disconnects from the network due to failure or other unforeseen circumstances.

- **Importance**: LWT helps maintain the reliability and consistency of data communication across MQTT clients. It ensures that other clients can be aware of the disconnection and can take appropriate actions or adjustments in response, maintaining the overall integrity and functionality of the system.

Setting up LWT

Configuring LWT involves specifying a will message and topic that the broker will publish if it detects an unexpected disconnection of the client. Here's how to set it up using the paho-mqtt client library:

- **Initialize the MQTT Client**: Create a new MQTT client instance and configure the LWT during this initialization.

```
import paho.mqtt.client as mqtt

def on_connect(client, userdata, flags, rc):
    print("Connected with result code "+str(rc))

# Setup LWT message and topic
will_topic = "clients/myclient/status"
will_message = "Disconnected unexpectedly"
will_qos = 1
will_retain = False

client = mqtt.Client()
client.on_connect = on_connect client.will_set(
                                 will_topic,
                                 will_message,
                                 qos=will_qos,
                                 retain=will_retain
                                 )
```

- **Connect to the MQTT Broker**: After setting up the LWT, connect the client to the MQTT broker.

```
client.connect("broker_address", 1883, 60)
client.loop_start()
# Start the network loop in a separate thread
```

- **Disconnect Normally** (Optional): If you disconnect normally, the LWT message will not be sent.

```
client.disconnect()
```

Practical Applications

Real-world applications of the LWT feature are varied and vital across many scenarios:

IoT Device Monitoring:

- **Scenario**: In an IoT ecosystem, devices periodically report their status to a monitoring system. If a device unexpectedly goes offline, LWT can alert the system to the disconnection.
- **Application**: The monitoring system can then alert technicians to check the device or can trigger failover mechanisms if necessary.

Home Automation Systems:

- **Scenario**: In smart homes, devices like thermostats, lights, and security cameras need to operate reliably. An unexpected disconnection could impact the home's environment or security.
- **Application**: LWT messages can be used to notify other devices or services in the home to take corrective action, such as switching to a default safe state.

Fleet Management:

- **Scenario**: Vehicles equipped with MQTT clients send real-time location and status data. If a vehicle's MQTT client disconnects unexpectedly, immediate action may be required.
- **Application**: The LWT message can trigger alerts to the fleet manage-

ment system to possibly reroute nearby vehicles or send assistance to the location last reported by the disconnected vehicle.

Using the LWT feature effectively enhances the reliability and robustness of MQTT-based systems, providing critical notifications that help maintain system integrity and responsiveness, particularly in applications where client availability and reliability are paramount.

Advanced Implementation Tips for MQTT in IoT Systems

Integration with System Architecture

Integrating MQTT's advanced features like QoS levels, retained messages, and Last Will and Testament (LWT) into an IoT system requires a thoughtful approach to both the technical and architectural aspects of the system. Here's how these features can be seamlessly integrated:

System Design and Planning:

- **Determine Requirements**: Assess the data criticality, network reliability, and device capabilities across your IoT ecosystem to define appropriate MQTT settings (QoS, LWT, etc.).
- **Service Layer Integration**: Integrate MQTT communication protocols within the service layer of your IoT architecture, ensuring that MQTT brokers are optimally positioned (possibly distributed) to manage messages efficiently.

Data Flow and Management:

- **Data Routing**: Use topic structures and retained messages to effectively route data to appropriate services and storage systems, enabling efficient data flow management.
- **State Management**: Design your system to handle state information

provided by LWT messages and retained messages, which can inform system components about device disconnections and last known configurations.

Security and Compliance:

- Ensure all communications are encrypted using TLS/SSL if sensitive data is transmitted.
- Implement proper authentication and authorization mechanisms to manage who can publish or subscribe to certain topics.

Troubleshooting Common Issues

Dealing with issues related to MQTT's advanced features involves understanding their root causes and addressing them systematically:

QoS Level Issues:

- **Symptoms**: Messages are not being received as expected, or there is excessive message duplication.

Diagnosis:

- Check the network stability and latency to ensure messages are transmitted within acceptable limits.
- Review MQTT client and broker logs to trace message flow and identify where losses or duplications occur.

Resolution:

- Adjust QoS levels appropriately based on the criticality and nature of the data.
- Ensure that clients and brokers are correctly implementing MQTT

specifications, particularly around message acknowledgments for QoS 1 and 2.

Retained Messages:

- **Symptoms**: Outdated or incorrect information is being received by new subscribers.

Diagnosis:

- Verify that publishers are updating retained messages correctly.
- Check for multiple publishers on the same topic that might be overriding each other's retained messages inappropriately.

Resolution:

- Implement a timestamp or version number within the retained message payload to identify outdated information.
- Set clear policies on who can publish retained messages to which topics.

Last Will and Testament (LWT):

- **Symptoms**: LWT messages are not being published as expected, or they are triggering false positives.

Diagnosis:

- Test client disconnections to ensure the broker recognizes and handles unexpected disconnections correctly.
- Check the configuration of LWT messages for correctness in terms of topic and payload.

Resolution:

- Adjust client keepalive and timeout settings to better match network conditions and client reliability.
- Update and test LWT settings regularly to ensure they reflect current system needs and configurations.

By implementing these integration and troubleshooting strategies, you can enhance the reliability, efficiency, and responsiveness of your IoT systems, leveraging MQTT's full capabilities to meet your specific operational requirements.

10

Chapter 10: Error Handling and Debugging

Common MQTT and JSON Errors

When working with MQTT and JSON in various applications, especially in IoT and data-intensive contexts, it's essential to be aware of common errors that can arise. Understanding these errors will help in developing more robust systems.

Overview of Common Errors

Errors in MQTT and JSON implementations typically relate to connectivity issues, data format discrepancies, and authorization problems, among others. These errors can disrupt normal operations and affect data integrity and application reliability.

MQTT Errors

Connection Failures:

- **Refused Connections**: This occurs when the MQTT broker refuses a connection attempt. Common reasons include providing incorrect client credentials (username/password), attempting to use an unsupported protocol version, or the broker being configured to deny connections under certain conditions (e.g., IP filtering).
- **Timeouts**: Connection attempts may timeout due to network issues, server overload, or incorrect network configurations. Ensuring network stability and proper server scaling can mitigate these issues.

Subscription and Publishing Issues:

- **Unauthorized Access**: If the client does not have the necessary permissions to subscribe to or publish on a particular topic, the broker will deny these operations. This can be managed through proper ACL (Access Control List) configurations on the broker.
- **Topic Filtering Issues**: Errors can occur if topics are not correctly formulated or if wildcards are used improperly. Clients might subscribe to broader or incorrect topics leading to either too much or too little data being received.

JSON Errors

Parsing Errors:

- **Malformed JSON**: Commonly arises when the JSON data structure is incorrect—missing quotes, braces, or commas. This results in a JSONDecodeError when using libraries like Python's json.
- **Incorrect Data Types**: Parsing errors may also occur if the expected data types are not matched (e.g., an integer is expected, but a string is found).

Serialization Errors:

- **Unsupported Data Types**: Not all Python data types can be directly serialized to JSON. For instance, tuples and datetime objects need to be converted to list or string formats, respectively, before serialization.
- **Deeply Nested Objects**: When objects are too deeply nested, some libraries might hit recursion limits during serialization, leading to errors.

Troubleshooting Tips

MQTT Troubleshooting:

- Always check the return codes provided by the MQTT broker during connection and publishing attempts; these can offer direct insights into what went wrong.
- Implement robust error handling and reconnection logic in your MQTT client to handle intermittent connectivity issues.

JSON Troubleshooting:

- Validate JSON payloads against a schema to ensure they meet the required structure and data types before parsing or sending.
- Use try-except blocks around JSON parsing and serialization code to catch and handle errors gracefully. Provide clear error messages or logs to aid in debugging.
- **General Best Practices**:
- Regularly update and patch MQTT broker and client software to fix known bugs and improve security.
- Develop and maintain comprehensive logging throughout the system to track down when and where failures occur.

Understanding these common MQTT and JSON errors and applying robust troubleshooting measures will enhance the stability and reliability of your applications, leading to smoother operations and a better user experience.

Debugging MQTT Connections

Effective debugging of MQTT connections is crucial for maintaining reliable data flow in IoT and other networked applications. By utilizing the right tools and techniques, you can quickly identify and resolve issues.

Tools and Techniques

Using MQTT Client Tools:

- **MQTT.fx**: A graphical tool that allows you to publish and subscribe to MQTT topics, making it easy to simulate client interactions and test broker behavior. It provides features like scripting support for automated testing and an intuitive interface for monitoring real-time data.
- **Mosquitto's Command-Line Clients (mosquitto_pub and mosquitto_sub)**: These tools are invaluable for quick tests and automations. They allow you to publish messages and subscribe to topics from the command line, which is helpful for scripting and integration into test environments.
- **Example Commands**:
- Publish: mosquitto_pub -h broker_address -t "topic/path" -m "message"
- Subscribe: mosquitto_sub -h broker_address -t "topic/path"

Logging and Monitoring:

- **Enabling Logging**: Most MQTT brokers, including Mosquitto, allow you to configure logging through their configuration files. Enable detailed logging to capture information about connections, subscriptions, and message flows.

· In Mosquitto, you can add the following lines to the mosquitto.conf file:

```
log_dest file /path/to/logfile
log_type all
```

· **Using Logs**: Logs provide a timestamped record of all broker activities, which is crucial for tracing the sequence of events leading up to an issue.

Step-by-Step Debugging Process

Identifying the Issue:

· **Connection Establishment**: Verify that the client can reach the broker. Common issues include network misconfigurations, incorrect broker addresses or ports, and firewalls blocking MQTT ports.
· **Message Delivery**: Check whether messages are being published and received as expected. Issues might involve QoS settings, topic mismatches, or payload problems.
· **Client Disconnections**: Determine if disconnections are happening unexpectedly. Potential causes include timeout settings, network instability, or client misconfigurations.

Analyzing Logs:

· **Isolate Relevant Entries**: Focus on the timestamps and log entries around the time the issue occurred. Filter logs by client ID or topic if possible to reduce noise.
· **Connection Logs**: Look for connection attempts, successes, and failures.

Pay attention to return codes provided by the broker, which can indicate the reason for connection problems.
- **Subscription and Publishing Logs**: Verify that subscribe and publish actions are succeeding. Look for acknowledgment messages from the broker or error messages related to these actions.
- **Error Codes and Messages**: MQTT brokers typically log error codes and messages that can directly point to the nature of the problem (e.g., unauthorized access, payload format errors).

Using External Monitoring Tools:

- Consider using network monitoring tools like Wireshark to capture and analyze MQTT packet flows. This can be particularly useful to see the actual data being sent and received, and to verify that the network layer is functioning correctly.

Reproducing the Issue:

- Try to reproduce the issue in a controlled environment. This can help isolate the variables involved and make it easier to test fixes.

Consult Documentation:

- Refer to the MQTT specification and your MQTT broker's documentation for insights into expected behaviors and configuration options. Often, solutions to common problems are well-documented.

By systematically applying these debugging steps and using the appropriate tools, you can efficiently diagnose and resolve issues in MQTT applications, leading to more stable and reliable operations.

Error Handling in Python Scripts

Error handling is a critical component of building robust applications, particularly in network-based operations like MQTT communications or when working with data formats like JSON. Python provides several mechanisms to handle errors gracefully, ensuring that your application can respond to unexpected issues effectively.

Python Error Handling Mechanisms

Try-Except Blocks:

- **Purpose**: Try-except blocks in Python are used to catch and handle exceptions (errors) that occur during the execution of a block of statements.
- **Usage**:

```
try:
    # Code that might throw an exception
    result = 10 / 0
except ZeroDivisionError:
    # Code that runs if an exception occurs
    print("Divided by zero!")
finally:
    # Code that runs no matter what
    print("This is executed after the try-except blocks.")
```

This example catches the ZeroDivisionError and prints an error message, preventing the application from crashing.

Custom Exception Classes:

- **Purpose**: Custom exceptions allow you to define and generate errors specific to your application's context, making your error handling more descriptive and targeted.
- **Creating Custom Exceptions**:

```
class MQTTConnectionError(Exception):
    """Custom exception for MQTT connection failures."""
    pass

class JSONValidationError(Exception):
    """Custom exception for JSON validation errors."""
    pass
```

- **Using Custom Exceptions**:

```
def connect_to_mqtt(broker):
    if not broker:
        raise MQTTConnectionError("Broker URL empty!")
    try:
        connect_to_mqtt("")
    except MQTTConnectionError as e:
        print(f"Connection failed: {e}")
```

Implementing Robust Error Handling

Reconnection Strategies:

- In the context of MQTT, handling disconnections gracefully is crucial. Implementing automatic reconnection logic can help maintain a stable connection.
- **Strategy**:

```
def on_disconnect(client, userdata, rc):
    if rc != 0:
        print("Unexpected disconnection. Reconnecting...")
        client.reconnect()

client = mqtt.Client()
client.on_disconnect = on_disconnect
client.connect("broker_address")
client.loop_forever()
```

- This setup uses the on_disconnect callback to detect unexpected disconnections and attempts to reconnect.

Data Validation:

- Validating JSON data before parsing (to prevent format errors) and after generation (to ensure data integrity) is critical.
- **Pre-Parsing Validation**:

```
import json

def validate_json(json_string):
    try:
        json.loads(json_string) # Attempt to parse JSON
    except json.JSONDecodeError:
        raise JSONValidationError("Invalid JSON format")
try:
    validate_json('{"name": "John Doe", "age": 30}')
except JSONValidationError as e:
    print(e)
```

· **Post-Generation Validation**:

```
def generate_json(data):
    json_string = json.dumps(data)
    validate_json(json_string) # Validate after generation
    return json_string
```

By incorporating these error handling mechanisms and strategies into your Python scripts, especially in environments where network stability and data integrity are paramount, you can significantly enhance the resilience and reliability of your applications. These practices ensure that your system can withstand and recover from a variety of operational issues.

Practical Error Handling Examples

Case Study: MQTT Connection Error Handling

Scenario: An MQTT client application frequently loses connection to the broker due to network instability, leading to missed messages and disrupted operations.

Debugging Approach:

- **Initial Observation**: Notice that the client disconnects frequently and does not attempt to reconnect automatically.
- **Logging and Monitoring**: Implement detailed logging around the connection logic to capture the frequency and circumstances of disconnections.
- **Identifying the Issue**: Analyze logs and confirm that disconnections are unexpected and happen during network instability.
- **Planning the Solution**: Decide to implement automatic reconnection with exponential backoff to handle intermittent network issues more gracefully.

Implemented Solution:

```
import time
import paho.mqtt.client as mqtt
def on_connect(client, userdata, flags, rc):
    if rc == 0:
        print("Connected successfully.")
    else:
        print("Connect failed with error code:", rc)
def on_disconnect(client, userdata, rc):
    if rc != 0:
        print("Unexpected disconnection.")
        attempt_reconnect(client)
def attempt_reconnect(client, attempt=1):
    wait_time = min(2 ** attempt, 300) # exponential
    backoff capped at 5 minutes time.sleep(wait_time)
    try:
        client.reconnect()
    except:
        print(f"Reconnect attempt {attempt} failed, retrying...")
        attempt_reconnect(client, attempt + 1)
client = mqtt.Client()
client.on_connect = on_connect
client.on_disconnect = on_disconnect
client.connect("broker_address", 1883, 60) client.loop_forever()
```

This code uses an exponential backoff strategy for reconnection attempts, which increases the wait time between attempts progressively, reducing the load on the network and broker.

Code Examples

- **Handling JSON Parsing Errors:**

```
import json

def parse_json(json_string):
    try:
        data = json.loads(json_string)
        print("JSON parsed successfully:", data)
        return data
    except json.JSONDecodeError as e:
        print(
                f"Failed JSON parse: {e.msg} at line {e.lineno},
                column {e.colno}"
            )

json_input = '{"name": "John Doe", "age": "thirty"}'
parse_json(json_input)
```

This function tries to parse a JSON string and handles any decoding errors by printing out a descriptive error message, including where the error occurred in the JSON string.

- **MQTT Connection Error Management:**

```
def connect_to_broker():
    client = mqtt.Client()
    client.on_connect = on_connect
    client.on_disconnect = on_disconnect

    try:
        client.connect("broker_address", 1883, 60)
        client.loop_start()
    except Exception as e:
        print("Connection failed:", e)
        attempt_reconnect(client)

connect_to_broker()
```

This example demonstrates a basic approach to handling MQTT connection attempts. If the connect method fails (due to network issues or incorrect broker details), it catches the exception and calls an attempt_reconnect function to try reconnecting.

Both examples emphasize the importance of robust error handling mechanisms in ensuring the reliability and resilience of applications using MQTT and JSON, critical for maintaining seamless operations in real-world scenarios.

Best Practices for Preventive Maintenance

Preventive maintenance in software development involves implementing practices that help prevent errors before they become problematic, ensuring systems remain reliable and perform optimally. Here's how you can apply these practices, particularly in environments that use MQTT and JSON.

Preventive Techniques

Unit Testing:

- **Importance**: Unit tests are crucial for verifying the functionality of individual parts of the application independently. They help catch errors early in the development cycle, preventing bugs from reaching production.

Examples:

- **MQTT Functionality**:

```
import unittest from my_mqtt_client
import MyMQTTClient
class TestMQTTClient(unittest.TestCase):

   def test_mqtt_connection(self):
   client = MyMQTTClient("broker_url")
   self.assertTrue(client.connect(), "Client should connect")

   def test_publish(self):
      client = MyMQTTClient("broker_url")
      client.connect()
      self.assertTrue(client.publish(
                     "topic/test",
                     "Hello World"
                     ),
                     "Message should publish"
                     )
```

- **JSON Functionality**:

```
import json
import unittest
class TestJSONFunctions(unittest.TestCase):
    def test_valid_json(self):
        json_string = '{"name": "John", "age": 30}'
        try:
            data = json.loads(json_string)
            self.assertEqual(data['name'], "John")
        except
            json.JSONDecodeError:
            self.fail("JSON decoding should not fail")


if __name__ == '__main__':
    unittest.main()
```

Continuous Integration (CI):

- **Role**: CI systems automate the testing and building of code. By integrating regularly, you can detect and solve errors quickly, which is especially crucial in dynamic environments using MQTT and JSON where data schemas and interfaces might frequently change.
- **Practice**: Set up CI pipelines to automatically run unit tests and integration tests whenever new code is committed. Tools like Jenkins, Travis CI, or GitHub Actions are commonly used for these purposes.

Monitoring and Alerts

System Monitoring Tools:

- **Introduction**: Monitoring tools can track the performance and health of applications, providing insights into how well the MQTT broker and JSON interfaces are functioning.

Tools:

- **For MQTT**: Use tools like HiveMQ's MQTT Inspector or MQTT Explorer to monitor MQTT traffic and visualize topic trees and client interactions.
- **For Systems**: Broader tools like Prometheus for metrics collection and Grafana for visualization can help monitor system metrics and logs.
- **Logs and Network Monitoring**: Tools like ELK Stack (Elasticsearch, Logstash, Kibana) or Splunk for logs and Wireshark for network traffic can offer deep insights into the system's operation.

Setting Up Alerts:

Guide:

- Identify critical thresholds and events that should trigger alerts. In MQTT, this could be frequent disconnections, high message drop rates, or unauthorized access attempts.
- Use monitoring tools to set up alerts. Most modern monitoring systems (like Prometheus with Alertmanager) allow you to define alert rules based on specific metrics or log entries.
- Integrate alert systems with communication channels such as emails, SMS, Slack, or other instant messaging platforms to ensure that the responsible parties are informed immediately about critical issues.

By adopting these preventive maintenance practices, you can significantly enhance the stability and reliability of your applications, reducing downtime and improving user satisfaction.

4

11

Chapter 11: Designing a Simple MQTT Server

Designing a Simple MQTT Server

Understanding MQTT Server Requirements

The MQTT server, commonly referred to as a broker, plays a central role in the MQTT ecosystem. It is responsible for managing network connections from MQTT clients, facilitating message exchanges by ensuring messages are appropriately published to subscribers, and maintaining the overall state and health of the messaging environment.

Server Role and Functions

Connection Management:

- The MQTT broker handles all incoming network connections from clients, establishing and maintaining sessions for each client. This involves managing client-specific settings such as keep-alive intervals and handling client disconnections and reconnections.

Message Distribution:

- **Publish/Subscribe Mechanism**: The broker receives messages published on specific topics and distributes these messages to clients that have subscribed to those topics. The broker must handle this efficiently to support potentially thousands of messages and subscriptions.
- **Quality of Service (QoS) Handling**: The broker is responsible for implementing the QoS policies for messages, which involves ensuring messages are delivered according to the level of service requested by the client (QoS 0, 1, or 2).

Session Management:

- For clients that connect with a clean session set to false, the broker must store session information, including subscriptions and potentially undelivered messages, which ensures continuity across client disconnections.

Security Management:

- Implementing standard security measures including client authentication (via username/password or certificates) and possibly authorization mechanisms to control access to topics.

Requirements Gathering

To design a simple MQTT server, consider the following typical requirements:

Handling Connections:

- The server must accept TCP/IP connections on the standard MQTT ports (1883 for non-TLS and 8883 for TLS-secured connections).
- Manage different client states and connection parameters, such as handling initial connection handshakes, managing keep-alive timeouts, and processing client disconnections.

Managing Topics:

- Efficient handling of topic subscriptions and unsubscriptions. This involves updating the list of subscriptions as clients subscribe to or unsubscribe from topics.
- Implementing a mechanism to efficiently route messages based on topic subscriptions.

Distributing Messages:

- Implement logic to handle different QoS levels for messages, ensuring that messages are stored, acknowledged, and retransmitted as necessary according to the QoS parameters.
- Ensuring the broker can handle high throughput and potential bursts of messages without significant delays or message loss.

Scalability and Performance:

- Design the server so that it can scale with an increasing number of connections and message throughput. This might involve optimizing data structures and algorithms for managing connections and subscriptions.
- Consider the use of in-memory databases or efficient data handling strategies to minimize latency and maximize throughput.

Reliability and Fault Tolerance:

- Incorporate mechanisms for fault tolerance, such as maintaining back-ups of client sessions and subscriptions or clustering brokers for high availability.

Security:

- Ensure the server supports essential security features such as TLS/SSL encryption for connections and provides capabilities for authentication and authorization.

Understanding these fundamental requirements will guide the development of a simple yet effective MQTT server capable of supporting a robust MQTT-based messaging system.

Choosing the Right Tools and Technologies

When building an MQTT server, especially one tailored for specific use cases or integrated within existing infrastructure, selecting the appropriate tools and technologies is crucial. Python, along with its rich ecosystem of libraries, offers a robust foundation for developing an MQTT server. Here's how to evaluate Python and its libraries for this purpose, along with considerations for integration.

Python and MQTT Libraries

Python:

Advantages:

- **Simplicity**: Python's straightforward syntax and readability make it an excellent choice for rapid development and maintenance.
- **Rich Library Ecosystem**: Python's comprehensive standard libraries and third-party modules can simplify many tasks associated with network programming, data handling, and integration.
- **Community Support**: Python has a large community and extensive documentation, which is beneficial for troubleshooting and improving your MQTT server.

Disadvantages:

- **Performance**: Python may not match the performance of compiled languages like C++ or Java, particularly in high-throughput scenarios due to its interpreted nature.

MQTT Libraries (paho-mqtt):

paho-mqtt:

- This is a widely used MQTT client library that provides features to connect, publish, and subscribe with an MQTT broker. While primarily a client library, paho-mqtt can be instrumental in testing the server or implementing custom client interactions within the server infrastructure.
- **Use Case**: While you cannot use paho-mqtt to build an MQTT server itself, it is invaluable for creating test clients or supplementary services that interact with your MQTT server.

Integration with Existing Infrastructure

Database Integration:

- **Use Case**: Storing persistent messages, logging data, or maintaining state information for clients.

Approach:

- Choose a database that matches your data structure and query needs (SQL for structured data with complex queries, NoSQL for scalability with simpler, more flexible data models).
- Utilize Python's database libraries (e.g., sqlite3, pymysql, pymongo) to integrate database operations seamlessly into your MQTT server logic.

Web Services Integration:

- **Use Case**: Incorporating real-time data into web applications, or managing MQTT server settings through web interfaces.

Approach:

- **REST API**: Develop a RESTful API for your MQTT server using frameworks like Flask or Django to handle HTTP requests. This can enable administrative tasks, such as monitoring, provisioning, or updating client subscriptions through web interfaces.
- **WebSocket Integration**: For real-time interaction with web clients, consider using WebSockets along with MQTT over WebSockets to provide a seamless, bidirectional communication channel.

Security Considerations:

- **Encryption**: Use SSL/TLS for encrypting MQTT and HTTP communications, which can be implemented using Python's ssl module or through external libraries and tools.

- **Authentication and Authorization**: Implement robust security mechanisms to control access to the MQTT server, which could include integrating with existing authentication services like OAuth, LDAP, or database-backed user management systems.

Testing and Deployment:

- Use tools like Docker for containerizing the MQTT server and its dependencies for easy deployment and scalability.
- Leverage continuous integration/continuous deployment (CI/CD) pipelines using tools like Jenkins or GitHub Actions to automate testing and deployment processes.

By carefully selecting the appropriate tools and technologies and considering how the MQTT server will integrate with existing systems, you can build a robust, efficient, and scalable solution that fits well within your technological ecosystem and meets your operational needs.

Architectural Design of an MQTT Server

Designing an MQTT server requires careful consideration of its architecture to ensure efficiency, scalability, and reliability. Here's an outline of the basic architecture and some strategies to handle scalability and reliability.

High-Level Architecture

Main Components:

- **Listener**: This component is responsible for accepting incoming network connections from MQTT clients. It needs to handle TCP/IP handshakes, initiate session creation, and manage continuous data reception.
- **Dispatcher**: Once messages are received and processed, the dispatcher

routes these messages to the appropriate subscribers based on the topic of the message. It also handles QoS requirements, ensuring messages are delivered according to the specified QoS level.

- **Storage System**:
- **Session and Subscription Management**: Stores session information for clients that choose persistent connections, as well as subscription details for each client.
- **Message Storage**: For QoS 1 and QoS 2 message delivery, storing messages that need to be redelivered is essential. This component also handles retained messages, storing the last known message for each topic that requires it.

Broker Engine:

- Central to the server, this component coordinates between the listener, dispatcher, and storage system. It processes connection requests, subscriptions, publish requests, and other MQTT-specific operations like ping requests.

Security Manager:

- Handles authentication and authorization for clients attempting to connect to the MQTT server. It ensures that clients are permitted to publish or subscribe to the specified topics.

Handling Scalability and Reliability

Threading:

- **Purpose**: To handle multiple client connections simultaneously, each client connection can be managed in a separate thread.
- **Implementation**: Use Python's threading module to manage multiple connections. This allows the server to maintain responsive interaction

with multiple clients even under heavy load.

Asynchronous Processing:

- **Purpose**: Enhances the server's ability to manage a large number of connections without being blocked by the I/O operations.
- **Tools**: Utilize Python's asyncio library or other asynchronous frameworks like Tornado or Twisted which are well-suited for handling numerous simultaneous network connections and asynchronous I/O operations.

Load Balancing:

- **Multiple Brokers**: Deploy multiple MQTT brokers and use a load balancer to distribute client connections among them. This not only increases the capacity of the system to handle more clients but also improves redundancy.
- **Client Load Distribution**: Implement client-side logic to connect to less loaded brokers based on some heuristic or server-side load reporting.

Fault Tolerance and Redundancy:

- **Replication**: Implement replication of session and message data across multiple servers or geographical locations. This ensures that if one server fails, another can take over without data loss.
- **Regular Backups**: Ensure that data within the MQTT server, especially persistent messages and client session information, is regularly backed up.

Monitoring and Logging:

- **System Monitoring**: Use tools to monitor system performance, including CPU usage, memory usage, and network I/O, to preemptively address bottlenecks or failures.
- **Logging**: Implement comprehensive logging across all components of the MQTT server. This will aid in diagnosing issues post-occurrence and for real-time monitoring of the system's health.

By designing your MQTT server with these architectural components and scalability strategies, you ensure that it can handle real-world usage scenarios efficiently and reliably. This foundational design allows for future expansions and optimizations specific to the needs of your applications and client base.

Security Design for an MQTT Server

Security in MQTT environments is critical, especially given the widespread use of MQTT in IoT applications which often involve sensitive or critical data. Here are key strategies to ensure robust security in terms of authentication, authorization, and data security.

Authentication and Authorization

Secure Connections Using TLS/SSL:

- **Purpose**: To encrypt data transmitted between MQTT clients and the broker, preventing eavesdropping and tampering.

Implementation:

- Configure the MQTT broker to require TLS for connections. This involves setting up a certificate authority (CA), server certificates, and possibly client certificates.
- Example for Mosquitto broker in mosquitto.conf:

```
port 8883
cafile /path/to/ca.crt
certfile /path/to/server.crt
keyfile /path/to/server.key
require_certificate true  # If client certificates are used
```

Handling Client Credentials:

- **Client Authentication**: Use username and password authentication as the simplest form. For enhanced security, consider requiring client certificates as part of the TLS handshake.

Authorization:

- Define topic-based access control lists (ACLs) to restrict which topics clients can publish to or subscribe from. This prevents unauthorized access to sensitive data and limits potential damage from compromised clients.
- Example ACL setup in Mosquitto:

```
acl_file /path/to/aclfile.acl
```

- In the ACL file:

```
user alice
topic readwrite home/alice/#
user bob
topic readonly home/bob/sensors/#
```

Data Security

Data Integrity and Confidentiality:

- **Encryption**: Ensure all data transmitted between clients and the broker is encrypted using TLS. This not only secures data in transit but also ensures that the data remains confidential and tamper-proof.
- **Message Signing**: Consider implementing additional message-level security measures such as digital signatures if ultra-high security is required. This can verify that messages have not been altered in transit.

Data Privacy:

- **Sensitive Data Handling**: Be cautious about what data is sent over MQTT. Avoid transmitting highly sensitive information like personal identifiers unless absolutely necessary. If such data must be sent, ensure it is encrypted and access is tightly controlled.
- **Retained Messages**: Handle retained messages with care, especially if

they contain sensitive data. Ensure that access to topics with retained messages is securely controlled, and consider periodically purging old messages.

Regular Security Audits:

- **Penetration Testing**: Regularly test your MQTT infrastructure for vulnerabilities, particularly focusing on authentication, authorization, and encryption implementations.
- **Security Audits**: Conduct periodic audits of your security policies and configurations to ensure they remain robust against emerging threats.

Compliance and Best Practices:

- **Compliance with Standards**: Ensure that your MQTT deployment complies with relevant standards and regulations, such as GDPR for data privacy or ISO/IEC standards for information security management.
- **Security Best Practices**: Follow best practices for IoT security, such as those recommended by OWASP or specific industry guidelines related to your application domain.

By integrating these security mechanisms, your MQTT server will be well-equipped to handle both general and sophisticated threats, ensuring that data remains secure and that the system integrity is maintained at all times.

12

Chapter 12:Implementing MQTT Server

Setting Up the Development Environment for an MQTT Server

To set up a robust development environment for building an MQTT server using Python and the paho-mqtt library, follow these step-by-step instructions. This setup will help you handle client communications effectively, although the actual MQTT broker functionality will need to be handled by a broker such as Mosquitto.

Installation of Required Packages

Install Python:

- Ensure that Python is installed on your system. You can download it from the official Python website. Most environments work well with Python 3.7 or newer.

Set Up a Virtual Environment (optional but recommended):

- It's a good practice to use a virtual environment for Python projects to manage dependencies effectively. You can set up a virtual environment by running:

```
python -m venv my_mqtt_env
```

Activate the virtual environment:

- On Windows:

```
my_mqtt_env\Scripts\activate
```

On macOS and Linux:

```
source my_mqtt_env/bin/activate
```

Install paho-mqtt:

- With your virtual environment activated, install the paho-mqtt Python package using pip:

```
pip install paho-mqtt
```

Additional Tools and Libraries (optional):

- For enhanced logging and debugging, you might consider installing additional packages like loguru for logging:

```
pip install loguru
```

- For JSON handling, Python's built-in json module is typically sufficient, but you can install simplejson for potentially better performance:

```
pip install simplejson
```

Initial Configuration

Basic MQTT Client Setup:

- Create a Python script to establish a basic MQTT client that can connect to an MQTT broker, subscribe to topics, and publish messages. Here's an initial setup example:

```
import paho.mqtt.client as mqtt
def on_connect(client, userdata, flags, rc):
    if rc == 0:
        print("Connected successfully.")
    else: print("Connect failed with error code", rc)

def on_message(client, userdata, msg):
    print(f"Received message: {
                        msg.payload.decode()
                        } on topic {msg.topic}")

client = mqtt.Client()
client.on_connect = on_connect
client.on_message = on_message

client.connect("localhost", 1883, 60)
client.subscribe("test/topic")

client.loop_start() # start the loop
```

Broker Configuration:

- If you are setting up a broker like Mosquitto on your local machine, ensure it's configured to accept connections. Modify the Mosquitto configuration file (mosquitto.conf) to allow anonymous access or set up user credentials.
- Start the Mosquitto broker:

```
mosquitto -c /path/to/mosquitto.conf
```

Environment Variables (optional):

- For production environments, consider setting up environment variables to manage configurations like broker URLs or credentials securely.
- Use Python's os module to access these environment variables:

```
import os
broker_url = os.getenv("MQTT_BROKER_URL", "localhost")
```

By following these steps, you'll establish a solid foundation for developing an MQTT server environment in Python, equipped with client capabilities and initial broker interaction. This setup allows you to simulate and handle client interactions and pave the way for building more complex MQTT-related functionalities.

Developing Core Functionalities for an MQTT Server

When developing an MQTT server, it's essential to focus on core functionalities such as connection management, topic subscription logic, and message handling. Here, we'll provide some conceptual outlines and example code snippets using Python to handle these functionalities, assuming the presence of an MQTT broker like Mosquitto for actual MQTT operations.

Connection Management

Handling incoming client connections and maintaining client states are crucial for the robustness of an MQTT server.

Code for Managing Client Connections:

- Example using Python's socket library to accept client connections:

```
import socket

server_socket = socket.socket(
                        socket.AF_INET,
                        socket.SOCK_STREAM
                        )
server_socket.bind(('0.0.0.0', 1883))# Bind to MQTT port
server_socket.listen()

while True:
    client_socket, addr = server_socket.accept()
    print(f"Connection from {addr}")
    # Handle the client connection in a separate thread or proc
```

Maintaining Client State:

This involves keeping track of each client's subscriptions, their QoS levels, and potentially any undelivered messages.

You would typically use a data structure or a database to store this information persistently, especially for supporting durable subscriptions (clients that expect to receive messages even after disconnections).

Topic Management

Managing topics involves implementing logic for clients to subscribe to topics and routing messages based on these subscriptions.

Topic Subscription Logic:

- Implementing subscription logic where clients can subscribe to topics with specific QoS levels.

```
subscriptions = {}
def subscribe(client_id, topic, qos):
    if topic not in subscriptions:
        subscriptions[topic] = []
    subscriptions[topic].append((client_id, qos))
    print(f"Client {client_id} subscribed to {topic} with QoS {qos}")
```

Message Routing:

- Routing published messages to all subscribed clients.

```
def publish(topic, message):
    if topic in subscriptions:
        for client_id, qos in subscriptions[topic]:
        # Send message to client from stored client_id and qos
        print(f"Sending message to {client_id} on topic {topic}")
```

Message Handling

Handling incoming messages, storing them if necessary, and distributing them to subscribers are fundamental operations.

Receiving Messages:

- Code to receive messages from a publisher and trigger the distribution logic.

```
def on_message_received(topic, message):
    print(f"Received message on {topic}")
    publish(topic, message) # Function defined in Topic Mngmnt
```

Storing Messages:

- For QoS levels 1 and 2, you might need to store messages until they are successfully delivered.
- Use a database or an in-memory data structure to temporarily store these messages.

Distributing Messages:

- Implementing the logic to distribute messages to all subscribers of a topic.

```
def distribute_message(topic, message):
  if topic in subscriptions:
     for client_id, _ in subscriptions[topic]:
        # Send message to each subscriber
        send_message_to_client(client_id, message)
```

These snippets provide a basic framework for developing the core function-alities of an MQTT server. Real-world implementations would need more robust error handling, scalability considerations, and integration with actual MQTT libraries or broker software to handle the MQTT protocol specifics effectively.

Implementing Security Features in an MQTT Server

Security is paramount in any networked application, especially for IoT devices communicating over MQTT. Here, we'll discuss how to implement TLS/SSL for encrypted connections and add client authentication mecha-nisms using usernames and passwords.

Integrating TLS/SSL

TLS (Transport Layer Security) provides a secure communication channel between clients and the server. Here's how to set up TLS in an MQTT environment:

Obtain SSL/TLS Certificates:

- You will need a server certificate and a private key, and possibly a CA (Certificate Authority) certificate if you're using CA-signed certificates. You can generate these using tools like OpenSSL or obtain them from a certificate authority.

Configuring the Broker:

- Using Mosquitto as an example, you need to configure it to use these certificates.
- Edit the mosquitto.conf file to include the following lines:

```
port 8883
cafile /path/to/ca.crt # Path to the CA certificate
certfile /path/to/server.crt # Path to the server certificate
keyfile /path/to/server.key # Path to the server's private key
```

Enabling TLS in the Broker:

Ensure that the broker listens on port 8883, which is standard for MQTT over TLS.

Restart the broker after making these changes to apply the new configuration.

Client Configuration:

Clients must also be configured to trust the CA that issued the server's certificate and to connect using TLS.

- Example using paho-mqtt in Python:

Adding Administrative Features to an MQTT Server

Effective administration of an MQTT server involves implementing compre-hensive monitoring and logging capabilities and providing tools for server management. These features are crucial for maintaining system health, optimizing performance, and ensuring security.

Monitoring and Logging

Server-Side Logging:

- **Purpose**: To capture and record significant events such as client connections, disconnections, message publications, and system errors.

Implementation:

- Configure the MQTT broker (e.g., Mosquitto) to log detailed information. This can be done by editing the mosquitto.conf file:

```
log_dest file /path/to/mosquitto.log
log_type all
```

- This setup instructs Mosquitto to log all types of events to a specified file, which includes debug information, errors, subscriptions, and publications.

Log Analysis:

- Regularly analyze the logs using tools like Logstash or Splunk to gain insights into usage patterns, detect potential issues, and monitor system health.
- Set up log rotation and archiving strategies to manage the size and number of log files, ensuring that logs do not consume excessive disk space and remain manageable and searchable.

Administration Tools

Topic Management:

- **Tools**: Develop or integrate tools that allow administrators to view, modify, and manage topic subscriptions and permissions. This could include:
- A web-based interface where administrators can see active topics, who is subscribed to what, and even modify topic ACLs (Access Control Lists).
- Scripts or command-line tools that can directly interact with the MQTT broker to manage topics and subscriptions.

Client Status Overview:

Dashboard:

Implement a dashboard using web technologies (HTML, CSS, JavaScript) possibly backed by a Python framework like Flask or Django. This dashboard could display real-time information about:

- Connected clients and their connection status.
- Volume of messages being published and subscribed to on various topics.
- Alerts and notifications on critical events like client disconnections or message publish failures.

Example of a basic Flask setup to display client status:

```
from flask import Flask, render_template
import paho.mqtt.client as mqtt

app = Flask(__name__)

# MQTT Setup
client = mqtt.Client()
client.connect("localhost", 1883, 60)

@app.route('/')

def index():
    # Assume 'get_client_status'
    # is a function that returns a list of client statuses
client_statuses = get_client_status()
return render_template('status.html', clients=client_statuses)

if __name__ == '__main__':
    app.run(debug=True)
```

System Alerts:

- **Purpose**: Implement mechanisms to alert administrators about critical conditions or errors.

Tools:

- Integrate MQTT with monitoring solutions like Prometheus and Grafana to trigger alerts based on specific metrics (e.g., unexpected client disconnections, high message latency).

- Use email or SMS notifications for critical alerts, ensuring administrators can respond to issues promptly.

By implementing these administrative features, you enhance the manageability of the MQTT server, ensure better operational oversight, and maintain high levels of system performance and security. These tools also help in complying with operational best practices and can significantly ease the burden of system maintenance.

13

Chapter 13: Testing and Validating the Server

Developing a Testing Strategy for an MQTT Server

A comprehensive testing strategy is essential for ensuring the reliability and robustness of an MQTT server. This strategy should include both unit testing of individual components and integration testing of the server as a whole. Here's how to approach these testing methodologies.

Unit Testing

Purpose:

To verify the functionality and correctness of individual components or modules of the MQTT server without interaction with any dependencies like databases or other external systems.

Tools and Frameworks:

- Use Python testing frameworks like unittest or pytest to create and run unit tests.
- Mock external dependencies using libraries such as unittest.mock or pytest-mock.

Example Tests:

- **Connection Management**: Test the ability of the server to handle incoming connections, manage disconnections, and maintain client state.

```python
import unittest
from unittest.mock import MagicMock
from mqtt_server import ConnectionManager

class TestConnectionManager(unittest.TestCase):
def test_handle_connection(self):
    manager = ConnectionManager()
    client = MagicMock()
    manager.handle_connection(client)
    client.connect.assert_called_once()

def test_handle_disconnection(self):
    manager = ConnectionManager()
    client = MagicMock()
    manager.handle_disconnection(client)
    client.disconnect.assert_called_once()

if __name__ == '__main__':
    unittest.main()
```

- **Message Routing**: Verify that messages published to specific topics are correctly routed to subscribed clients.

```
class TestMessageRouting(unittest.TestCase):
def test_route_message(self):        .
    router = MessageRouter()
    client = MagicMock()
    router.subscribe(client, 'test/topic')
    router.route_message('test/topic', 'Hello')
    client.receive.assert_called_with('Hello')
```

Integration Testing

Purpose: To test the server as a whole, including its interactions with clients, to ensure all parts work together as expected.

Approaches:

- **End-to-End Testing**: Simulate real-world scenarios where multiple clients connect, subscribe, publish, and receive messages.
- **Stress Testing**: Evaluate how the server performs under heavy loads, such as high numbers of connections or a large volume of messages.

Tools:

- Use real MQTT clients or tools like paho-mqtt in Python to simulate client behavior.
- Tools like MQTT.fx or Mosquitto's command-line utilities (mosquitto_pub and mosquitto_sub) can be used to manually test various scenarios.

Example Integration Test:

- Test that the server correctly handles multiple clients subscribing to the same topic and receiving messages.

```
def test_multiple_subscriptions():
    client1 = mqtt.Client()
    client2 = mqtt.Client()
    client1.connect('localhost', 1883, 60)
    client2.connect('localhost', 1883, 60)
    client1.subscribe('common/topic')
    client2.subscribe('common/topic')
    # Simulate sending a message to 'common/topic'
    publish_to_topic('common/topic', 'Test message')
    # Check both clients receive the messageassert
    client1.received_message == 'Test message'assert
    client2.received_message == 'Test message'
```

Execution and Monitoring

- **Continuous Integration**: Integrate testing into a CI pipeline to automatically run tests every time changes are made. Tools like Jenkins, Travis CI, or GitHub Actions can facilitate this.
- **Monitoring**: Use tools to monitor test executions and collect results, ensuring that issues are caught and addressed promptly.

By developing a thorough testing strategy that covers both unit and integration aspects, you ensure that the MQTT server is robust, performs well under different conditions, and behaves as expected in real-world scenarios.

Testing Tools and Techniques for an MQTT Server

Testing an MQTT server effectively involves a combination of tools and strategies that simulate client interactions, measure server responsiveness, and ensure stability under varying load conditions. Here's how to utilize MQTT client tools for simulation and conduct stress testing.

Using MQTT Client Tools

- **Purpose**: To simulate realistic client interactions with the MQTT server, helping validate server functionality and performance.

Tools:

- **MQTT.fx**: A graphical tool that allows for subscribing, publishing, and scripting MQTT messages. Useful for manual testing and exploring MQTT topics.
- **Mosquitto's Command-Line Tools** (mosquitto_pub and mosquitto_sub): These are ideal for automated testing environments where you can script a series of publish and subscribe actions.
- Example command to publish messages:

```
mosquitto_pub -h localhost -t 'test/topic' -m 'Hello World' -q 1
```

- Example command to subscribe to topics:

```
mosquitto_sub -h localhost -t 'test/topic'
```

Usage Scenarios:

- **Functional Testing**: Test specific features like QoS, retained messages, or clean session behaviors.
- **Concurrency Testing**: Simulate multiple clients connecting, subscribing, and publishing simultaneously to assess how well the server handles multiple connections.

Stress Testing

- **Purpose**: To determine the server's performance and stability under high load, particularly its ability to handle a large number of connections and messages without performance degradation or failure.

Strategies:

- **Incremental Load Increase**: Gradually increase the number of simulated clients and messages until the server shows signs of strain or failure. This helps identify the maximum capacity of the server.
- **Sustained High Load**: Maintain a high load for an extended period to test the endurance of the server and uncover issues like memory leaks or resource exhaustion.

Tools:

- **JMeter**: Originally designed for web applications but also supports MQTT via plugins. It can simulate large numbers of clients and high message throughput.
- **Gatling**: While primarily for HTTP, it can be extended to support MQTT with custom scripts. Gatling offers detailed performance reporting.

Example Stress Test Setup:

- Configure JMeter or a similar tool to simulate hundreds or thousands of clients publishing and subscribing to multiple topics.
- Monitor server metrics like CPU, memory, and network usage during the test to identify performance bottlenecks and stability issues.

Considerations:

- **Resource Monitoring**: Use system monitoring tools to track server resource usage during the tests. Tools like Prometheus or Grafana can provide real-time metrics visualization.
- **Robust Logging**: Ensure that logging is sufficiently detailed to diagnose issues post-test. This includes logs for connection handling, message processing, and error reporting.

Best Practices

- **Automate Testing**: Where possible, automate the testing processes to ensure that they can be repeated consistently and run as part of a continuous integration pipeline.
- **Document Findings**: Keep a detailed record of the testing scenarios, configurations, and results to help diagnose issues and plan for future scaling needs.
- **Regular Testing**: Conduct these tests regularly and especially after significant changes to the MQTT server configuration or code to ensure ongoing stability and performance.

By employing these testing tools and techniques, you can ensure that your MQTT server is not only functional but also robust enough to handle real-world operating conditions effectively.

Deployment Considerations for an MQTT Server

Deploying an MQTT server in a production environment requires careful planning to ensure reliability, security, and scalability. Here are some deployment best practices and tips for maintaining and updating your MQTT server effectively.

Deployment Best Practices

Choose the Right Hosting Environment:

- Consider the expected load, network latency, and geographical location of your clients when choosing a hosting solution. Options include on-premises servers, cloud providers (like AWS, Azure, or Google Cloud), or hybrid environments.

Secure Configuration:

- **Encrypt Communication**: Ensure that TLS/SSL is enabled for all communications between clients and the server. This protects data integrity and privacy.
- **Use Strong Authentication and Authorization Mechanisms**: Implement robust client authentication methods, such as username/password, certificates, and possibly integrate with existing identity management systems.
- **Access Control**: Define strict ACLs (Access Control Lists) to manage who can publish or subscribe to specific topics.

Redundancy and Failover:

- Deploy multiple MQTT broker instances to provide redundancy. Configure them in a failover cluster to ensure high availability. Tools like Kubernetes can automate the deployment and scaling of containerized

MQTT broker instances.

Performance Tuning:

- Configure your MQTT broker to optimize performance based on your specific use case. This might involve tuning parameters related to message throughput, session persistence, and client handling.

Automated Backups:

- Schedule regular backups of important configuration files and data, especially for brokers handling persistent messages or maintaining durable client sessions.

Maintaining and Updating the Server

Routine Maintenance:

- Regularly check and optimize the server's performance through monitoring tools. Address any emerging issues such as memory leaks, increasing response times, or bandwidth bottlenecks.

Software Updates:

- Keep the MQTT broker software up to date with the latest patches and releases. Regular updates help secure your server against known vulnerabilities and often provide performance improvements and additional features.
- Plan and schedule updates during off-peak hours to minimize disruption. Use staging environments to test new updates before rolling them out in production.

Monitoring and Alerts:

- Implement comprehensive monitoring to track the health and perfor-mance of the MQTT server. Use tools like Prometheus for monitoring metrics and Grafana for visualizing those metrics in real-time.
- Set up alerting mechanisms to notify administrators of critical con-ditions, such as server outages, high memory usage, or unauthorized access attempts.

Documentation and Change Management:

- Maintain detailed documentation of the server configuration, deploy-ment architecture, and operational procedures. This is crucial for troubleshooting and ensuring that all team members understand the system setup.
- Use a change management system to track modifications to the server or its configuration. This helps in auditing and can assist in trou-bleshooting by identifying when and how changes might have affected the system.

Regular Security Audits:

- Conduct periodic security audits to ensure that the MQTT server con-forms to best security practices and complies with relevant regulatory re-quirements. Address any vulnerabilities or compliance issues promptly.

By adhering to these deployment and maintenance best practices, you can ensure that your MQTT server operates reliably and securely in a production environment, supporting the critical needs of your applications and users efficiently.

14

Chapter 14: Persistent Storage with SQLite

Introduction to Persistent Storage for MQTT Servers

Persistent storage is a critical component for maintaining robust MQTT server operations, especially in scenarios where reliability and message integrity are paramount. Understanding the need for persistence and choosing the right storage solution are essential steps in designing an effective MQTT architecture.

Need for Persistence

Retaining Messages:

- **Purpose**: MQTT servers need to store messages that are published with the QoS level 1 or 2 to ensure they are delivered even after network failures or client disconnections. Additionally, messages published with the "retain" flag must be kept until they are explicitly replaced or deleted to ensure new subscribers immediately receive the last known value upon subscription.

- **Impact**: Without persistent storage, any retained messages or undelivered QoS messages would be lost in the event of a server restart or failure, potentially leading to incomplete data transmission and state inconsistency across clients.

Managing Subscriptions:

- **Client Sessions**: Persistent storage helps manage client sessions, especially for clients that connect with the "clean session" flag set to false. The server needs to remember the client's subscriptions so that it can continue to deliver appropriate messages when the client reconnects after a disconnection.
- **Durable Connections**: For applications requiring high reliability, such as industrial IoT systems where sensor data must be consistently monitored, maintaining these subscriptions across server restarts is crucial.

Choosing SQLite

Lightweight:

- **Resource Efficiency**: SQLite is renowned for its minimal resource footprint, making it ideal for environments where server performance and low overhead are crucial. It doesn't require a separate server process, integrating directly into the MQTT server application as a simple library.
- **Simplicity**: Unlike more complex database systems that require extensive setup, configuration, and maintenance, SQLite can be set up with minimal effort.

Reliability:

- **ACID Compliance**: SQLite transactions are ACID-compliant, ensuring that all operations are processed reliably and any changes are saved consistently, which is particularly important for retaining messages and subscription information securely.
- **Data Integrity**: With features like journaling, SQLite ensures that the database is not corrupted, even in cases of application crash or power failures.

Ease of Integration:

- **API Availability**: SQLite is supported by a vast range of programming languages, including Python, which is commonly used for MQTT server scripts. This makes it easy to integrate directly into existing MQTT server implementations.
- **Portability**: SQLite databases are stored in a single file, simplifying data backup, migration, and management.

Use Cases:

- Suitable for systems where large-scale transactions are not required but where ease of deployment, configuration, and maintenance are preferred.
- Ideal for both development and production environments of small to medium-scale MQTT deployments.

Implementation Example

Setting up SQLite for MQTT message retention could involve creating tables to store message data and subscriptions:

```
CREATE TABLE retained_messages (
                        topic TEXT PRIMARY KEY,
                        payload BLOB,
                        qos INTEGER,
                        retain BOOLEAN
              );

CREATE TABLE client_subs(
                    client_id TEXT,
                    topic TEXT
                    qos INTEGER,
                     PRIMARY KEY (client_id, topic)
                    );
```

These tables can then be used to store and retrieve messages and sub-scriptions as needed by the MQTT broker, ensuring data persistence across sessions and server restarts.

Integrating SQLite with MQTT Server

SQLite is an excellent choice for MQTT servers due to its simplicity, reliability, and ease of integration. Below are the detailed steps for setting up SQLite in a Python environment and designing a database schema that effectively supports MQTT functionalities.

Setting Up SQLite

Install SQLite Library:

- In Python, SQLite is supported natively through the sqlite3 module, which is included in the Python Standard Library. Thus, no additional installation is necessary for SQLite itself. However, for enhanced functionality or more complex operations, you might consider additional libraries like sqlalchemy.

Using SQLite in Python:

- To start using SQLite, simply import the sqlite3 library and connect to a database. Here's a basic setup:

```
import sqlite3

# Connect to SQLite database, file is created if it does not exist
connection = sqlite3.connect('mqtt_server.db')
cursor = connection.cursor()

# Create a table as part of the setup process
cursor.execute(
''' CREATE TABLE IF NOT EXISTS clients (
                                client_id TEXT PRIMARY KEY,
                                client_status TEXT NOT NULL
                                )
''')

connection.commit()

# Closing the connection when done
connection.close()
```

Database Schema Design

For an MQTT server, your database schema needs to accommodate various types of data, including client information, subscriptions, and retained messages. Below is a proposed schema:

Clients Table:

- Stores information about each client, such as their ID and status.

```
CREATE TABLE IF NOT EXISTS clients (
                    client_id TEXT PRIMARY KEY,
                    client_status TEXT NOT NULL
                    );
```

Subscriptions Table:

- Maintains records of topic subscriptions along with the client ID and the QoS level.

```
CREATE TABLE IF NOT EXISTS subscriptions (
                    client_id TEXT,
                    topic TEXT,
                    qos INTEGER,
                    PRIMARY KEY (
                            client_id,
                            topic
                            ),
                    FOREIGN KEY (client_id)
                    REFERENCES clients (client_id)
                    ON DELETE CASCADE
);
```

Retained Messages Table:

- Keeps track of messages that need to be retained on specific topics, including the message payload and its QoS.

```
CREATE TABLE IF NOT EXISTS retained_messages (
                        topic TEXT PRIMARY KEY,
                        payload BLOB,
                        qos INTEGER
              );
```

Implementing Basic Operations

Inserting Data:

- Add a new client or update an existing client's status.

```
def add_or_update_client(client_id, status):
    with sqlite3.connect('mqtt_server.db') as conn:
        cursor = conn.cursor()
        cursor.execute(
        ''' INSERT INTO clients (client_id, client_status) VALUES (?, ?)
        ON CONFLICT(client_id) DO UPDATE SET
        client_status = excluded.client_status;
        ''', (client_id, status))

    conn.commit()
```

Querying Data:

· Retrieve all subscriptions for a given client.

```
def get_subscriptions(client_id):
    with sqlite3.connect('mqtt_server.db') as conn:
        cursor = conn.cursor()
        cursor.execute(
        'SELECT topic, qos FROM subscriptions
        WHERE client_id = ?', (client_id,))
        return cursor.fetchall()
```

Handling Retained Messages:

· Insert or update a retained message.

```
def set_retained_message(topic, payload, qos):
    with sqlite3.connect('mqtt_server.db') as conn:
        cursor = conn.cursor()
        cursor.execute('''
            INSERT INTO retained_messages (topic, payload, qos)
            VALUES (?, ?, ?) ON CONFLICT(topic)
            DO UPDATE SET payload = excluded.payload,
                                    qos = excluded.qos;
        ''', (topic, payload, qos))

    conn.commit()
```

By integrating SQLite, your MQTT server can effectively manage data related to clients, subscriptions, and messages, ensuring robust operation even across server restarts and maintaining a high level of service integrity.

Implementing Data Operations with SQLite in an MQTT Server

Properly managing data operations in an MQTT server requires a robust approach to CRUD (Create, Read, Update, Delete) operations and a strong emphasis on data integrity and transaction management. Here's how you can implement these aspects using SQLite in a Python environment.

CRUD Operations

Create (Insert):

- Insert new data into tables for clients, subscriptions, and retained messages. Handle new client connections and topic subscriptions efficiently.

```
def insert_client(client_id, status):
    with sqlite3.connect('mqtt_server.db') as conn:
        cursor = conn.cursor()
        cursor.execute(''' INSERT INTO clients (
                                        client_id,
                                        client_status
                                        )
                        VALUES (?, ?) ''', (client_id, status)
                        ) conn.commit()

def insert_subscription(client_id, topic, qos):
    with sqlite3.connect('mqtt_server.db') as conn:
        cursor = conn.cursor()
        cursor.execute(''' INSERT INTO subscriptions (
                                            client_id,
                                            topic,
                                            qos
                                            )
                        VALUES (?, ?, ?) ''', (client_id, topic, qos)
                        )
conn.commit()
```

Read (Select):

- Retrieve data from the database, such as fetching all subscriptions for a specific client or retrieving the retained messages for a topic.

```
def get_client_status(client_id):
    with sqlite3.connect('mqtt_server.db') as conn:
        cursor = conn.cursor()
        cursor.execute(
            'SELECT client_status FROM clients
            WHERE client_id = ?', (client_id,)
            )
        return cursor.fetchone()

def get_retained_message(topic):
    with sqlite3.connect('mqtt_server.db') as conn:
        cursor = conn.cursor()
        cursor.execute(
                'SELECT payload, qos FROM retained_messages
                WHERE topic = ?', (topic,)
                )
        return cursor.fetchone()
```

Update:

· Modify existing records, such as updating client status or changing a subscription's QoS.

```
def update_client_status(client_id, new_status):
    with sqlite3.connect('mqtt_server.db') as conn:
        cursor = conn.cursor()
        cursor.execute(
                ''' UPDATE clients SET client_status = ?
                WHERE client_id = ? ''', (new_status, client_id)
                )

conn.commit()
```

Delete:

- Remove records from the database, such as deleting a client's subscriptions when they disconnect permanently.

```
def delete_client(client_id):
    with sqlite3.connect('mqtt_server.db') as conn:
        cursor = conn.cursor()
        cursor.execute(
            'DELETE FROM clients
            WHERE client_id = ?', (client_id,)
            )

conn.commit()
```

Data Integrity and Transactions

Transaction Management:

Use transactions to ensure that changes to the database are performed atomically. This means either all operations within the transaction are completed successfully, or none are applied in the event of an error.

- SQLite supports transactions natively through the BEGIN TRANSACTION, COMMIT, and ROLLBACK statements.

```
def add_client_with_subscription(client_id, status, topic, qos):
    with sqlite3.connect('mqtt_server.db') as conn:
        try: cursor = conn.cursor()
            cursor.execute('BEGIN TRANSACTION')
            cursor.execute(
                    ''' INSERT INTO clients (
                                        client_id,
                                        client_status
                                        )
                        VALUES (?, ?) ''', (client_id, status)
                        )
            cursor.execute(
                    ''' INSERT INTO subscriptions (
                                        client_id,
                                        topic,
                                        qos
                                        )
                        VALUES (?, ?, ?) ''', (client_id, topic, qos)
                        )
            cursor.execute('COMMIT')
        except Exception as e:
    cursor.execute('ROLLBACK')
    raise e
```

Error Handling:

- Proper error handling ensures that the system can gracefully recover from unexpected situations, maintaining database integrity and application stability.
- Always handle exceptions, especially during transactions, to ensure that a rollback is triggered if necessary.

By following these practices, you can ensure robust data operations in your MQTT server, supporting critical functionalities like maintaining client states, managing subscriptions, and ensuring that messages are retained correctly. These operations are fundamental to the reliable performance of the MQTT server, especially in production environments.

Testing and Validation for MQTT Servers with SQLite Integration

Testing the persistence features of an MQTT server and ensuring that SQLite is properly integrated are essential for ensuring system reliability and data integrity. Here's how to effectively test these features and troubleshoot common issues.

Testing Persistence

Simulating Server Restarts:

- **Objective**: Ensure that data (e.g., client states, subscriptions, retained messages) persists across server restarts as expected.

Method:

- Run the MQTT server and populate it with test data, including various client connections, subscriptions, and retained messages.
- Shut down the server and restart it.
- Verify that all data is still accurately represented and that clients can resume operations without needing to re-establish previously made subscriptions.

Ensuring Data Consistency:

- **Data Integrity Checks**: After operations that modify the database (insert, update, delete), validate the integrity and consistency of the data.
- Use assertions in unit tests to check database states against expected values.

Example:

```
def test_subscription_persistence():
    insert_subscription('client1', 'topic/a', 1)
    # Restart the server simulation
    restart_server_simulation()
    subscriptions = get_subscriptions('client1')
    assert subscriptions == [
                            (
                                'client1',
                                'topic/a',
                                1
                            )
                            ],
                            "Sub should persist after restart"
```

Automated Regression Testing:

- Implement automated tests that run frequently (e.g., nightly) to ensure that updates to the server do not introduce bugs that affect persistence.

Troubleshooting Common Issues

Database Locking Issues:

- **Symptom**: Slow performance or errors related to database access, especially in write-heavy environments.

Troubleshooting:

- Ensure that database connections are properly closed after transactions.
- Use finer-grained transactions to reduce the duration of locks.
- Consider configuring SQLite for higher concurrency if defaults are not sufficient.

Data Corruption:

- **Symptom**: Unexpected data loss or corruption.

Troubleshooting:

- Regularly back up the database and test the restoration process.
- Use journaling features in SQLite (e.g., WAL mode) to enhance data recovery options.
- Check for disk space issues or hardware faults that might cause database corruption.

Performance Bottlenecks:

- **Symptom**: The server responds slowly, especially as the number of clients or the volume of messages increases.

Troubleshooting:

- Optimize SQL queries and use indexes where applicable to speed up data retrieval.
- Profile the server to identify and address performance bottlenecks in the application code or database access patterns.

Migration Issues:

- **Symptom**: Errors or data loss when upgrading the database schema.

Troubleshooting:

- Develop a clear migration strategy that includes scripting all schema changes.
- Test schema migrations in a staging environment before applying them in production.
- Ensure all migrations are reversible to allow quick rollback in case of issues.

Incorrect Data Retrieval:

- **Symptom**: Applications retrieve outdated or incorrect data.

Troubleshooting:

- Verify that all read operations correctly handle the database's transaction isolation levels.
- Ensure that queries are correctly formulated and test them individually.

By implementing rigorous testing and effective troubleshooting methodologies, you can ensure that your MQTT server with SQLite integration operates reliably and efficiently, maintaining high standards of performance and data integrity.

15

Chapter 15: Handling Concurrent Connections

Understanding Concurrent Connections in an MQTT Server

Managing concurrent client connections effectively is crucial for the performance and reliability of an MQTT server. Here, we'll explore the challenges posed by concurrency and different models for handling these challenges.

Challenges of Concurrency

Resource Contention:

- **Description**: Multiple clients attempting to access or modify shared resources (like message queues or subscription lists) simultaneously can lead to conflicts or resource contention.
- **Impact**: This can degrade performance, cause delays in message delivery, or lead to inconsistent data states if not managed correctly.

Scalability Limits:

- **Description**: As the number of concurrent connections increases, the server's ability to handle additional connections and messages without a drop in performance can be strained.
- **Impact**: This can result in slower response times, increased latency, and potential service outages under high load.

Complexity in State Management:

- **Description**: Maintaining the state of each connection (e.g., connected, subscribed topics, undelivered messages) becomes more complex as the number of clients grows.
- **Impact**: Errors in state management can lead to lost messages or clients being wrongly subscribed or unsubscribed from topics.

Concurrency Models

Different models can be adopted to handle concurrency in MQTT servers, each with its strengths and limitations.

Threading:

- **Description**: Uses multiple threads to handle client connections simultaneously, allowing for parallel processing of client requests.
- **Pros**:
- Relatively easy to implement and understand.
- Effective in scenarios with I/O-bound tasks, as threads can handle multiple waiting operations simultaneously.
- **Cons**:
- Overhead of context switching and potential for thread contention.
- Requires careful synchronization to avoid issues like race conditions and deadlocks.

Multiprocessing:

- **Description**: Employs multiple processes instead of threads, each with its own memory space, to handle client connections.
- **Pros**:
- Avoids the pitfalls of threading related to shared memory because processes do not share memory space.
- Can take full advantage of multi-core processors to truly run operations in parallel.
- **Cons**:
- Higher memory usage due to duplication of memory for each process.
- More complex inter-process communication (IPC) compared to threading.

Asynchronous I/O (Asynchronous Programming):

- **Description**: Uses non-blocking I/O operations and event loops to manage multiple connections within a single thread/process.
- **Pros**:
- Efficient handling of a large number of connections with minimal overhead.
- Reduces complexity associated with multi-threading and is naturally suited for I/O-bound and high-latency operations.
- **Cons**:
- Steeper learning curve due to the non-linear style of programming.
- Debugging can be more challenging because of the event-driven nature.

Practical Application

- **Choosing a Model**: The choice of concurrency model depends on the specific requirements and constraints of your MQTT server. For instance:
- Use **threading** if you need a simple solution with moderate scalability

and your server is mostly I/O-bound.

- Opt for **multiprocessing** if you have CPU-intensive tasks and sufficient hardware resources.
- Consider **asynchronous I/O** if you expect a high number of concurrent connections and need to manage them with high efficiency and low overhead.
- **Implementation Tools**:
- For **asynchronous I/O**, Python's asyncio library provides a powerful framework for asynchronous network programming.
- For **threading** and **multiprocessing**, Python's threading and multiprocessing libraries respectively offer robust options.

Concurrent client management is a critical aspect of MQTT server architecture that impacts its scalability, performance, and reliability. Choosing and implementing the right concurrency model is key to building a robust MQTT server.

Implementing Concurrency Handling in an MQTT Server

When it comes to managing concurrent connections in an MQTT server, choosing the right concurrency model is crucial. The decision should align with the server's performance requirements, expected load, and the nature of the tasks it performs. Here, we discuss how to make this choice and delve into implementing asynchronous I/O using Python's asyncio library.

Choosing a Model

Assessment of Requirements:

- **Connection Density**: High numbers of concurrent client connections favor models that handle large-scale I/O operations efficiently, such as asynchronous I/O.
- **Task Type**: CPU-bound tasks might benefit from multiprocessing to

leverage multiple CPU cores, whereas I/O-bound tasks are well-suited to threading or asynchronous I/O.

- **Resource Availability**: Consider the server's resource availability (e.g., memory, CPU). Multiprocessing requires more memory because it duplicates resources across processes.

Specific Reasons to Choose a Model:

- **Threading**:
- Chosen for moderate levels of concurrency with tasks that involve waiting, such as I/O operations, due to its ease of implementation and effective use of I/O waiting time.
- **Multiprocessing**:
- Ideal for CPU-intensive operations where tasks can be completely isolated and run in parallel without interfering with each other.
- **Asynchronous I/O**:
- Best for high connection counts and I/O-bound operations, particularly when minimal overhead and high efficiency are required.

Using Asynchronous I/O with asyncio

asyncio is a Python library that provides infrastructure for writing single-threaded concurrent code using coroutines, multiplexing I/O access over sockets and other resources, running network clients and servers, and other related primitives. Here is a guide to implementing an MQTT server that handles connections asynchronously:

Basic Setup:

- Install an MQTT library that supports asyncio, such as hbmqtt or integrate asyncio with paho-mqtt using bridges.
- Set up an asyncio event loop to manage asynchronous tasks.

Implementing Async Server:

- **Connection Handler**:

```
import asyncio
import socket async
def handle_client(reader, writer):
    data = await reader.read(100) # Read up to 100 bytes
    message = data.decode()
    addr = writer.get_extra_info('peername')

    print(f"Received {message} from {addr}")
    writer.close() # Close the connectionasync

def main():
    server = await  asyncio.start_server(
                            handle_client,
                            '127.0.0.1', 8883
                            )
    addr = server.sockets[0].getsockname()
    print(f'Serving on {addr}')

    async with server:
        await server.serve_forever()

asyncio.run(main())
```

Handling MQTT Operations:

- Integrate MQTT operations within the handle_client coroutine. Operations like connecting, subscribing, publishing, and disconnecting should be handled asynchronously within this coroutine.

Error Handling:

- Use try-except blocks around awaitable operations to manage exceptions effectively, ensuring the server remains stable and responsive even when errors occur.

Performance Optimization:

- Use asyncio features like Tasks, Futures, and Events to fine-tune operation timings and resource management.

Testing and Validation:

- Employ tools like aiohttp test suite to simulate client requests and ensure the server handles all operations as expected.

By carefully implementing asynchronous I/O in your MQTT server, you can achieve excellent scalability and efficiency, particularly in environments with high numbers of concurrent client connections. This approach allows for handling multiple connections on a single thread, minimizing context switching and making efficient use of server resources.

Scalability Considerations for an MQTT Server

Scalability is a critical factor for MQTT servers, especially when expected to manage thousands of concurrent connections in environments like IoT, where devices continuously communicate their state or receive commands. Here, we'll explore effective techniques for scaling MQTT servers, focusing on load balancing and clustering.

Scaling with Concurrent Connections

Optimizing Connection Handling:

- **Connection Pooling**: Use connection pooling to manage and reuse connections efficiently. This reduces the overhead of continuously creating and destroying connections, which can be resource-intensive.
- **Tuning Operating System Parameters**: Adjust OS-level parameters such as the maximum number of file descriptors and TCP socket tuning parameters to handle more connections simultaneously.

Asynchronous Communication:

- Implement asynchronous communication mechanisms to handle multiple connections on fewer threads. As discussed previously, libraries like asyncio can manage thousands of connections on a single thread by using non-blocking I/O operations.

Resource Allocation:

- Ensure that the MQTT server has enough resources (CPU, memory, bandwidth) to handle the expected load. Use dynamic resource allocation and auto-scaling environments (e.g., Kubernetes) to adjust resources based on demand.

Load Balancing and Clustering

Load Balancing:

- **Purpose**: Distributes client connections and requests across multiple server instances, preventing any single server from becoming a bottleneck.
- **Techniques**:

- **Hardware Load Balancers**: Use dedicated hardware to route traffic to the least loaded server.
- **Software Load Balancers**: Implement software solutions like HAProxy or Nginx to distribute connections. These tools can analyze traffic and apply various algorithms (round-robin, least connections, IP-hash, etc.) to distribute load effectively.

Clustering:

- **Purpose**: Increases the capacity of the MQTT system by allowing multiple servers to work together as a single logical unit.
- **Implementation**:
- **Broker Clustering**: Many advanced MQTT brokers support clustering out-of-the-box. This setup involves configuring multiple MQTT brokers to share state and workload, making the cluster appear as a single broker to clients.
- **Session Persistence**: Use centralized storage or distributed caches (like Redis) to share session and state information across the cluster. This ensures that any broker in the cluster can serve any client based on the shared state.

Example Architectural Setup:

- **Initial Setup**: Deploy multiple MQTT broker instances behind a load balancer. Configure each broker to connect to a centralized session database or a distributed cache.
- **Client Distribution**: Configure the load balancer to distribute incoming client connections across the brokers evenly or based on custom rules that suit the deployment scenario.
- **State Sharing**: Implement mechanisms to synchronize state across brokers, such as retained messages or client session states, using a distributed cache.

Failover and Redundancy:

- Ensure that the system can handle the failure of one or more brokers without affecting the overall system's availability. Use techniques such as automatic failover where if one broker fails, its clients are quickly reconnected to another broker in the cluster.

Best Practices

- **Regular Benchmarking and Testing**: Continuously monitor and test the system under various loads to identify bottlenecks and adjust configurations accordingly.
- **Scalable Infrastructure**: Consider using cloud services that offer easy scalability options to dynamically adjust resources as the load on your MQTT server changes.
- **Security Considerations**: Ensure that load balancers and cluster nodes are secured to prevent unauthorized access and data breaches, especially when handling sensitive information.

By employing these scalability considerations, your MQTT server can handle increasing loads efficiently, maintaining high availability and performance even under high concurrency scenarios.

Performance and Stress Testing for MQTT Servers

Ensuring that your MQTT server can handle high loads and perform efficiently under pressure is crucial. This involves conducting targeted stress tests and employing robust monitoring tools to optimize performance. Below, we detail how to approach testing for concurrency and the best practices for monitoring and optimizing server performance.

Testing for Concurrency

Stress Testing:

- **Objective**: Stress tests are designed to push the system to its limits and beyond, to evaluate its performance under extreme conditions. For an MQTT server, this typically means simulating many clients connecting, subscribing, publishing, and receiving messages simultaneously.

How to Conduct:

- **Setup**: Use tools like MQTT.fx, JMeter, or custom scripts that can create a large number of MQTT client connections and generate message traffic. Configure these tools to incrementally increase the number of simultaneous connections and message rates.
- **Execution**: Run the tests while systematically increasing the load to observe how the server behaves under stress. Monitor for how the server handles connection drops, message delivery, and system crashes.

Parameters to Test:

- Maximum number of concurrent connections.
- Throughput (messages per second) at different Quality of Service (QoS) levels.
- Latency in message delivery as load increases.

Automation:

- Integrate these stress tests into an automated CI/CD pipeline to regularly assess the performance impact of new code changes or configurations.

Monitoring and Optimization

Monitoring Tools:

- **Built-in MQTT Monitoring**: Some MQTT brokers come with built-in monitoring capabilities that can provide metrics on current connections, throughput, and other performance indicators.

External Monitoring Tools:

- **Prometheus and Grafana**: Use Prometheus to collect metrics and Grafana for visualization. Set up Prometheus to scrape metrics exposed by the MQTT server or its ecosystem, and use Grafana to create dashboards that visualize these metrics in real-time.
- **Elastic Stack**: For more detailed logging and performance data, integrate an Elastic Stack (Elasticsearch, Logstash, Kibana) to collect, search, and visualize server logs and performance metrics.

Optimization Techniques:

- **Identifying Bottlenecks**:
- Use the collected data from monitoring tools to identify performance bottlenecks, such as high CPU usage, memory leaks, or I/O bottlenecks.

Resource Allocation:

- Adjust server resource allocation based on identified needs, such as increasing memory limits or optimizing database interactions.

Code Profiling:

- Employ profiling tools to understand the runtime behavior of the server. Tools like Python's cProfile or Py-Spy can help identify inefficient code paths or functions that consume excessive resources.

Best Practices for Optimization:

- **Caching Frequently Accessed Data**: Implement caching mechanisms for frequently accessed data, such as retained messages or commonly used topic filters.
- **Database Optimization**: Optimize database queries and indexes, especially for operations that log or retrieve message data and client sessions.
- **Load Balancing**: Distribute client connections and data across multiple server instances or nodes to balance the load and reduce the risk of any single point of failure.

Regular Reviews and Adjustments:

- Continuously review the performance data and adjust the system configurations, resource allocations, and scaling strategies based on the latest insights and observed trends.

By rigorously testing for concurrency and employing a comprehensive strategy for monitoring and optimization, you can ensure that your MQTT server remains robust, scalable, and capable of handling high loads effectively. This proactive approach not only enhances the server's performance but also improves overall system reliability and user satisfaction.

16

Chapter 16: Performance Optimization

Profiling Server Performance for an MQTT Server

Profiling server performance is crucial for understanding how an MQTT server behaves under different workloads, identifying bottlenecks, and optimizing for better performance. Here's a detailed look at the key performance metrics to monitor and the tools that can be used for effective profiling.

Performance Metrics

To effectively monitor and optimize an MQTT server, you should focus on several key performance metrics:

Throughput:

- **Description**: Measures the number of messages processed per unit of time. It's crucial for assessing how well the server handles message delivery and reception.
- **Metrics**: Messages per second sent and received.

Latency:

- **Description**: Time taken for a message to travel from publisher to subscriber. It's vital for applications requiring real-time performance.
- **Metrics**: Average, median, and 95th percentile latencies.

Connection Handling:

- **Description**: The server's ability to handle connections and disconnections, especially under high loads.
- **Metrics**: Connection establishment and tear-down rates per second.

Resource Utilization:

- **CPU Usage**: Percentage of CPU utilized by the MQTT server.
- **Memory Usage**: Amount of RAM used by the server.
- **Disk I/O**: Disk operations related to persistent message storage and logging.

Error Rates:

- **Description**: Tracks the rate of failed message deliveries, dropped connections, or any protocol violations.
- **Metrics**: Errors per minute or per session.

Concurrency Levels:

- **Description**: Measures the number of concurrent connections sustained over time.
- **Metrics**: Number of active connections at any given time.

Profiling Tools

For an in-depth analysis of an MQTT server's performance, various tools can be employed:

Built-in Broker Tools:

- Many MQTT brokers offer built-in metrics and logging capabilities. For example, Mosquitto provides verbose logging options that can be analyzed for performance insights.

Monitoring and Observability Tools:

- **Prometheus**: Collects and stores its metrics as time series data, allowing for powerful querying and alerting. Used in conjunction with:
- **Grafana**: Provides visualization capabilities for the data collected by Prometheus. You can create dashboards that display key performance metrics in real-time.

Logging Analysis Tools:

- **Elastic Stack (ELK)**: Elasticsearch, Logstash, and Kibana can be used together to collect, store, and visualize logs from the MQTT server, which can be useful for identifying patterns or issues.

Network Monitoring Tools:

- **Wireshark**: Captures and analyzes packets on the network, allowing you to see MQTT traffic in detail. This is useful for troubleshooting and understanding message flows.
- **ntopng**: Provides real-time network traffic monitoring and is useful for detecting network-related performance bottlenecks.

Profiling Libraries for Code-Level Insights:

- **Python Profilers** (for MQTT servers implemented in Python):
- **cProfile**: A built-in Python profiler that provides detailed information about function calls and execution times.
- **Py-Spy**: A sampling profiler for Python applications that can run without interrupting the running program. It's excellent for understanding performance without the overhead typically associated with profiling.

Stress Testing Tools:

- **JMeter**, **Gatling**, and **Locust**: These tools can simulate high loads on the MQTT server and are instrumental in performance tuning exercises.

Best Practices for Profiling

- **Regular Profiling**: Integrate profiling and monitoring into your regular maintenance routines to catch performance degradation early.
- **Contextual Analysis**: Always analyze performance metrics in the context of your specific server use case. Different applications may have different performance sensitivities.
- **Performance Baselines**: Establish performance baselines to quickly identify when the server's performance deviates from expected parameters.

By employing these metrics and tools, you can gain a comprehensive understanding of your MQTT server's performance, leading to targeted optimizations that enhance overall system efficiency and reliability.

Optimizing Server Configuration for an MQTT Server

Ensuring optimal performance in an MQTT server involves both code-level optimizations in Python and strategic tweaks in server configuration. Here's how to approach these enhancements effectively.

Optimizing Python Code

Efficient Use of Data Structures:

- **Choice of Data Structures**: Use the most appropriate data structures for your tasks. For example, use deque from the collections module for fast appends and pops from both ends, which is ideal for queues.
- **Avoiding Redundancy**: Reduce memory usage by avoiding redundant data storage and using generators where feasible instead of fully materialized lists.

Algorithm Optimization:

- **Complexity Reduction**: Focus on reducing the time complexity of your algorithms. For instance, if your operations involve searching elements frequently, consider using sets or dictionaries which offer average $O(1)$ time complexity for lookups.
- **Loop Optimizations**: Minimize the overhead inside critical loops and eliminate unnecessary loop iterations.

Profiling and Refactoring:

- Use Python's built-in tools like cProfile to identify bottlenecks. Refactor the parts of the code that consume the most time or resources based on profiling results.

Example:

```
import cProfile
import pstats
def main_function():
    # Example function that needs profiling
    pass

if __name__ == "__main__":
    profiler = cProfile.Profile()
    profiler.enable()
    main_function()
    profiler.disable()
    stats = pstats.Stats(profiler).sort_stats('cumtime')
    stats.print_stats()
```

Concurrency Handling:

- Utilize asyncio for asynchronous programming to handle I/O-bound tasks efficiently. This can significantly improve the performance of network communications and I/O operations.

Server Configuration Tweaks

Network Settings:

- **Connection Handling**: Increase the number of allowable concurrent connections if your server is expected to handle many simultaneous connections. This might involve adjusting the OS-level settings for maximum open file descriptors.
- **TCP Optimizations**: Implement TCP tuning parameters such as increas-

ing buffer sizes (tcp_rmem, tcp_wmem), and enable TCP_NODELAY if the latency is critical.

MQTT Broker Configuration:

- **Message Throughput**: Increase max_inflight_messages to allow more QoS 1 and QoS 2 messages to be in flight simultaneously without being acknowledged.
- **Persistence Options**: If using persistent storage, optimize how often data is written to disk. Some brokers allow configuring the persistence interval which can significantly affect performance.

Database Accesses:

- **Connection Pooling**: Implement connection pooling for database accesses to reduce the overhead of establishing database connections frequently.
- **Query Optimization**: Use prepared statements and optimize SQL queries to minimize database access times. Ensure indexes are used effectively to speed up query processing.

Caching:

- **Implement Caching**: Use caching mechanisms to store frequently accessed data, such as user sessions or frequently accessed topics. Tools like Redis can be integrated for fast in-memory caching.

Load Balancing:

- **Use Load Balancers**: Deploy load balancers to distribute client connections and requests evenly across multiple server instances or cores, which can help manage higher loads more efficiently.

Logging and Monitoring:

- **Optimize Logging**: While comprehensive logging is crucial for diagnosing issues, excessive logging can degrade performance. Adjust logging levels appropriately (e.g., avoid verbose logging in production unless troubleshooting).

Continuous Optimization

- **Regular Review and Testing**: Continuously monitor performance metrics and conduct regular stress testing to identify new optimization opportunities.
- **Stay Updated**: Keep the software dependencies, Python itself, and any third-party libraries used up to date, as updates often include performance improvements and security enhancements.

By adhering to these best practices in code optimization and server configuration, you can significantly enhance the performance and scalability of your MQTT server, ensuring it remains robust and efficient under various operational conditions.

Advanced Optimization Techniques for MQTT Servers

Optimizing an MQTT server for high performance involves implementing advanced techniques like caching mechanisms and parallel processing. These strategies can dramatically reduce load times, enhance throughput, and decrease response latency.

Caching Mechanisms

Purpose of Caching:

- Caching is used to temporarily store frequently accessed data in memory, reducing the need to repeatedly fetch this data from slower storage systems like disks or databases.

Implementing Caching:

- **Local In-Memory Caching**:
- Use Python's in-built data structures like dictionaries to cache data directly within the application. This is particularly effective for storing frequently accessed configurations or temporary data that does not need to persist between restarts.
- Example using a dictionary for caching user sessions:

```
session_cache = {}

def get_user_session(user_id):
    if user_id in session_cache:
        return session_cache[user_id]
    session = database_fetch_session(user_id)
    # Hypothetical function
    session_cache[user_id] = session
    return session
```

Distributed Caching Systems:

Use distributed caching systems like Redis or Memcached when scaling horizontally across multiple servers or when caching large volumes of data.

- Example integrating Redis with Python for caching MQTT topic sub-scriptions:

```
import redis

redis_client = redis.StrictRedis(
                        host='localhost',
                        port=6379,
                        db=0
                        )

def cache_subscriptions(user_id, subscriptions):
    redis_client.set(user_id, json.dumps(subscriptions))

def get_cached_subscriptions(user_id):
    result = redis_client.get(user_id)
    if result:
        return json.loads(result)
    return None
```

Cache Eviction Policies:

Implement eviction policies to manage memory usage efficiently. Common policies include Least Recently Used (LRU), First In First Out (FIFO), and Time To Live (TTL) for entries.

Parallel Processing

Purpose of Parallel Processing:
   Parallel processing is used to distribute processing tasks across multiple processors or machines, thereby reducing the processing time and improv-

ing application throughput.

Techniques for Parallel Processing:

Multiprocessing:

Use Python's multiprocessing library to distribute work across multiple processes. This is useful for CPU-bound tasks where the GIL (Global Interpreter Lock) might be a bottleneck.

- Example of using multiprocessing to handle multiple client connections:

```
from multiprocessing

import Pool

def handle_client(client_info):
    # Process client data
    pass

if __name__ == '__main__':
    client_data = [client1, client2, client3]
    # List of client data
    with Pool(processes=4) as pool:
        results = pool.map(handle_client, client_data)
```

Asynchronous Programming:

Use asyncio for managing I/O-bound tasks, allowing you to handle thousands of connections in a non-blocking way.

- Example of asynchronous client handling:

```
import asyncio

async def handle_client(reader, writer):
    data = await reader.read(100)
    print(f"Received: {data.decode()}")

async def main():
    server = await asyncio.start_server(
                                handle_client,
                                '127.0.0.1',
                                8883
                                )
await server.serve_forever()

asyncio.run(main())
```

Thread Pooling:

- Utilize thread pools to manage threading overhead and reuse threads efficiently. Python's concurrent.futures.ThreadPoolExecutor is effective for this purpose.

Best Practices

- **Monitoring and Profiling**: Regularly monitor and profile server performance to identify which areas benefit most from caching and parallel processing.
- **Scalability Testing**: Continuously test scalability to ensure that caching

and parallel processing implementations effectively handle increased loads.

- **Consistency Management**: In parallel processing environments, ensure data consistency across threads or processes, especially when caching mutable data.

By implementing these advanced optimization techniques, you can significantly enhance the efficiency and performance of your MQTT server, ensuring it can handle high loads and concurrent operations smoothly.

Continuous Monitoring and Maintenance of MQTT Servers

For MQTT servers, which are critical components in IoT and data communication ecosystems, continuous monitoring and systematic maintenance are essential to ensure reliability, performance, and security. Here's how to implement robust monitoring solutions and effective routine maintenance practices.

Implementing Monitoring Solutions

Setting Up Monitoring Systems:

- **Purpose**: Continuous monitoring helps detect and diagnose runtime problems, assess system health, and optimize performance based on real-time data.

Tools and Techniques:

System Metrics Monitoring:

- Use tools like **Prometheus** to collect system metrics such as CPU usage, memory usage, network I/O, and disk I/O.
- Configure **Grafana** dashboards to visualize these metrics, allowing for easy interpretation of data trends and quick detection of anomalies.

Application Performance Monitoring (APM):

- Implement APM solutions such as **New Relic** or **Datadog** for more detailed insight into the MQTT server's operations, such as transaction times, error rates, and throughput.

Log Management:

- Utilize log aggregation and analysis tools like **Elastic Stack (ELK)** or **Splunk** to collect and analyze server logs. This is vital for troubleshooting and understanding behavioral patterns.

Custom MQTT Metrics:

- Track MQTT-specific metrics such as the number of active connections, subscription counts, message rates (published and received), and message latencies.
- Use MQTT broker's built-in support for metrics or develop custom monitoring hooks if needed.

Notification and Alert Systems:

- Integrate alerting mechanisms within monitoring tools to send notifications via email, SMS, or communication platforms like Slack when critical thresholds are breached (e.g., high CPU usage, low disk space, or service downtime).

Routine Maintenance Practices

Maintenance Scheduling:

- Establish a routine maintenance schedule that does not conflict with peak usage times. Plan for maintenance activities during off-peak hours to minimize impact on users.

Performance Tuning:

- Regularly analyze performance data collected through monitoring tools to identify potential bottlenecks or inefficiencies.
- Tune server configurations (e.g., network settings, database optimizations) and scale resources (e.g., adding more CPU or memory) based on observed demands and performance metrics.

Software Updates:

- Keep the MQTT server software and its dependencies up-to-date with the latest security patches and performance improvements.
- Test updates in a staging environment before deploying them to production to ensure compatibility and prevent disruptions.

Database Management:

- Regularly back up important data, especially data related to client configurations, retained messages, and persistent sessions.
- Perform periodic database optimizations such as reindexing, vacuuming (in systems like PostgreSQL), or garbage collection to ensure efficient data retrieval and storage.

Disaster Recovery Planning:

- Develop and regularly update a disaster recovery plan. This plan should include procedures for data restoration, server redeployment, and quick switch-over to backup systems in case of critical system failures.

Documentation and Training:

- Maintain detailed documentation of the server configuration, deployment architecture, and maintenance procedures. This is crucial for effective troubleshooting and maintenance.
- Provide training sessions for team members on handling routine maintenance tasks and responding to alerts.

By implementing these monitoring and maintenance strategies, you can ensure that your MQTT server operates reliably, performs optimally, and can quickly recover from unexpected failures or load spikes. Continuous monitoring coupled with proactive maintenance not only enhances server uptime but also ensures that performance and security standards are consistently met.

17

Chapter 17: Advanced Client Features

Implementing Auto-Reconnect in MQTT Clients

Auto-reconnect is a critical feature for MQTT clients, particularly in environments where network stability cannot be guaranteed. This feature ensures that the client remains connected or promptly attempts to reconnect following a network interruption, thus maintaining consistent communication and data integrity. Below, we explore why auto-reconnect is essential, how to implement it, and how to test it effectively.

Need for Auto-Reconnect

Maintaining Persistent Connections:

- In MQTT, the continuity of connections is crucial for ensuring messages are delivered reliably. Auto-reconnect helps maintain these connections, especially for clients that subscribe to topics where messages might be lost during disconnections.

Handling Unstable Network Environments:

- In scenarios where network instability is common (e.g., mobile networks, remote areas), auto-reconnect is vital for resuming operations without manual intervention, which is critical for IoT devices deployed in the field.

Enhancing User Experience:

- For applications dependent on real-time data (e.g., real-time monitoring systems), ensuring a persistent connection via auto-reconnect significantly enhances the user experience by reducing downtime and data gaps.

Designing the Auto-Reconnect Feature

Using the paho-mqtt library in Python, the auto-reconnect mechanism can be efficiently implemented. Here's an outline of the logic and structure:

Basic Setup:

- Utilize the on_disconnect callback provided by paho-mqtt to detect disconnections.
- Implement a reconnection strategy within this callback.

Implementation Example:

```
import time
import paho.mqtt.client as mqtt

def on_connect(client, userdata, flags, rc):
    if rc == 0:
        print("Connected successfully.")
    else:
        print(f"Failed to connect, return code {rc}")

def on_disconnect(client, userdata, rc):
    print("Disconnected from the broker")
    # Attempt to reconnect unless client disconnect deliberate
    if rc != mqtt.MQTT_ERR_SUCCESS:
        auto_reconnect(client)
```

```
def auto_reconnect(client, interval=5):
    while True:
        try:
            print("Attempting to reconnect...")
            if client.reconnect() == 0:
                print("Reconnected successfully.")
                break
            else:
                time.sleep(interval)
        except Exception as e:
            print(f"Reconnect failed: {e}")
            time.sleep(interval)

client = mqtt.Client() client.on_connect = on_connect
client.on_disconnect = on_disconnect
client.connect("mqtt.example.com", 1883, 60)
client.loop_start()
```

Testing Auto-Reconnect

Testing the auto-reconnect feature involves simulating network failures to ensure the client can recover from various disconnection scenarios:

Network Failure Simulation:

- Use network simulation tools or firewall rules to artificially disrupt the network connection between the client and the MQTT broker.
- Tools like comcast (Linux) or network conditioner features (on iOS and macOS) can simulate network issues.

Test Scenarios:

- **Complete Network Failure**: Simulate a total loss of network connectivity.
- **Intermittent Connectivity**: Simulate a network that frequently and irregularly drops and re-establishes connectivity.
- **High Latency and Packet Loss**: Simulate conditions where packets are significantly delayed or lost.

Automated Testing:

- Integrate the testing of the auto-reconnect feature into an automated test suite using tools like Python's unittest framework.
- Implement test cases that assert the client's ability to reconnect and resume normal operations after a disconnection.

Monitoring and Validation:

- During testing, monitor logs and use MQTT utilities to verify that messages continue to flow correctly after reconnections. Confirm that no data is lost or duplicated, and subscriptions remain active.

By implementing and thoroughly testing an auto-reconnect feature, you ensure that your MQTT clients can handle network instabilities gracefully, maintaining reliable communication and enhancing overall system robustness.

Implementing Scheduling in MQTT Clients

Scheduling tasks in MQTT clients is crucial for applications that require regular updates, such as telemetry data collection, automated control messages, or routine status updates. Effective scheduling ensures that messages are sent and actions are taken at precise intervals, maintaining system integrity and efficiency.

Introduction to Scheduling

Importance of Scheduling:

- **Regular Updates**: Regularly scheduled tasks are essential for applications that depend on timely data updates, such as temperature monitoring or stock level updates in IoT systems.
- **Resource Efficiency**: Scheduling helps manage resource use efficiently, ensuring that the network and server are not overwhelmed by uneven bursts of data.
- **Reliability and Consistency**: Automated scheduling ensures that operations happen consistently and reliably, without relying on external triggers or manual intervention.

Using sched or APScheduler

For implementing scheduling in Python MQTT clients, sched provides a simple, in-built option, whereas APScheduler offers more flexibility and features.

Using sched:

- The sched module is a straightforward scheduler included in Python's standard library, suitable for smaller or less complex scheduling needs.
- Example of using sched to schedule MQTT publishing:

```
import sched
import time
import paho.mqtt.client as mqtt

scheduler = sched.scheduler(time.time, time.sleep)

def publish_message(client, topic, message):
    client.publish(topic, message)
    print(f"Published message to {topic}: {message}")
    # Schedule the next call
    scheduler.enter(
                    60, 1, publish_message,
                    (client, topic, message)
                    )
    client = mqtt.Client()
    client.connect("mqtt.example.com", 1883, 60)
    client.loop_start()

# Schedule the first call scheduler.enter(
                    60, 1, publish_message,
                    (client, "sensor/data", "Hello MQTT")
                    )
scheduler.run()
```

Using APScheduler:

APScheduler is a powerful, feature-rich scheduler that supports multiple scheduling strategies (cron, interval, and delay), making it ideal for more complex scenarios.

· Example of using APScheduler for periodic MQTT tasks:

```
from apscheduler.schedulers.background
import BackgroundScheduler import paho.mqtt.client as mqtt

def publish_message(client, topic, message):
    client.publish(topic, message)
    print(f"Published message to {topic}: {message}")

client = mqtt.Client()
client.connect("mqtt.example.com", 1883, 60)
client.loop_start()

scheduler = BackgroundScheduler()
scheduler.add_job(
                    publish_message,
                    'interval',
                    minutes=1,
                    args=(client, "sensor/data", "Hello MQTT")
                    )
scheduler.start()
```

Best Practices and Error Handling

Best Practices:

- **Task Overlap**: Ensure that scheduled tasks do not overlap in a way that could cause resource contention or data corruption.
- **Logging and Monitoring**: Implement logging for all scheduled tasks to monitor their execution and outcome. Use monitoring tools to track the performance and reliability of tasks.
- **Time Synchronization**: Ensure that the client system's clock is synchronized with an authoritative time source to avoid drifts that could affect scheduling.

Error Handling:

- **Resilience**: Implement error handling within each scheduled task to manage failures gracefully. For example, retry mechanisms or error notifications can help address temporary issues.
- **Resource Cleanup**: Ensure that resources like network connections or file handles are properly managed and cleaned up even when errors occur.
- **Exception Handling**: Use try-except blocks to catch and log exceptions in scheduled tasks, preventing one failed task from affecting others.

By integrating robust scheduling capabilities into MQTT clients and adhering to best practices in implementation and error handling, you can enhance the functionality, reliability, and efficiency of your MQTT applications.

Enhancing Client Security in MQTT Applications

Security is paramount in MQTT applications, especially when dealing with sensitive data or operating in environments susceptible to cyber threats. Enhancing client security involves implementing advanced measures such as sophisticated encryption techniques, secure key management practices, and certificate-based authentication. Here's how to bolster the security of

MQTT clients:

Advanced Security Features

Advanced Encryption:

- Beyond standard TLS/SSL encryption, consider implementing additional encryption layers for message payloads, especially for highly sensitive data.
- **End-to-End Encryption (E2EE)**: Ensures that messages are encrypted at the source and decrypted only by the intended recipient, not even by the MQTT broker.

Secure Key Management:

- Proper management of encryption keys is critical to maintaining data security.
- **Hardware Security Modules (HSMs)**: Use HSMs to generate, store, and handle cryptographic keys securely.
- **Key Rotation Policies**: Regularly rotate encryption keys and certificates to mitigate the risks associated with key compromise.

Certificate-Based Authentication:

- Utilize X.509 certificates for client authentication, which is more secure than traditional username and password methods.
- **Public Key Infrastructure (PKI)**: Implement a PKI to manage issuance, renewal, and revocation of certificates effectively.

Implementing Enhanced Security

Here's a step-by-step guide on incorporating these advanced security enhancements into an MQTT client setup:

Setting Up Certificate-Based Authentication:

- **Obtain Certificates**: Obtain client certificates from a trusted Certificate Authority (CA) or your own PKI.

Configure MQTT Client:

```
import paho.mqtt.client as mqtt
def on_connect(client, userdata, flags, rc):
   if rc == 0:
      print("Connected with result code "+str(rc))
   else:
      print("Failed to connect, return code "+str(rc))

client = mqtt.Client()
client.tls_set(
            ca_certs="ca.crt",
            certfile="client.crt",
             keyfile="client.key",
             tls_version=ssl.PROTOCOL_TLSv1_2
            )
client.on_connect = on_connect

client.connect("mqtt.example.com", 8883, 60)
client.loop_forever()
```

This setup ensures the connection is encrypted and authenticated using TLS with the MQTT broker.

Implementing End-to-End Encryption:

Encryption Logic:

Encrypt the payload before sending and decrypt upon reception.

- Use libraries like pycryptodome to handle encryption.

```python
from Crypto.Cipher import AES
import base64
def encrypt_payload(data, key):
    cipher = AES.new(
                    key,
                    AES.MODE_EAX) ciphertext,
            tag = cipher.encrypt_and_digest(data.encode('utf-8')
            )
    return base64.b64encode(
                    cipher.nonce + tag + ciphertext
                    ).decode('utf-8'
                    )
def decrypt_payload(encrypted_data, key):
    data = base64.b64decode(encrypted_data) nonce,
    tag,
    ciphertext = data[:16],
    data[16:32],
    data[32:] cipher = AES.new(key,
                        AES.MODE_EAX,
                        nonce=nonce
                        )
    return
    cipher.decrypt_and_verify(ciphertext, tag).decode('utf-8')
```

- Ensure the encryption keys are securely exchanged or managed using a key management service.

Key Management:

- **Key Storage**: Utilize secure storage solutions such as HSMs or encrypted key vault services to store cryptographic keys.
- **Automate Key Rotation**: Implement automated mechanisms to rotate keys and update corresponding configurations without manual intervention.

Best Practices and Error Handling

- **Validate Certificate Chains**: Always verify the certificate chain up to the CA to ensure the legitimacy of certificates.
- **Regular Security Audits**: Regularly audit security configurations and practices to identify and rectify vulnerabilities.
- **Error Handling**: Implement robust error handling in your security mechanisms to gracefully handle security exceptions and maintain system stability.

By adopting these advanced security measures, you ensure that your MQTT clients are well-protected against various security threats, maintaining the integrity and confidentiality of your data across the network.

18

Chapter 18: Interacting with Multiple Brokers

Multi-Broker Architecture for MQTT Clients

Using multiple MQTT brokers in a network can significantly enhance the performance, reliability, and scalability of MQTT deployments. Here, we'll explore the benefits of employing a multi-broker setup and provide insights on architectural considerations for designing MQTT clients that can effectively manage connections to multiple brokers.

Benefits of Using Multiple Brokers

Improved Reliability and Fault Tolerance:

- By distributing the client connections across multiple brokers, the over-all system is less susceptible to failure. If one broker goes down, clients can automatically reconnect to another broker, thereby maintaining continuous service availability.

Enhanced Load Distribution:

- A multi-broker architecture helps in balancing the load more effectively. Client requests can be distributed across several brokers based on factors like geographic location, connection load, or topic-specific configurations. This distribution helps prevent any single broker from becoming a bottleneck.

Increased Scalability:

- Scaling the MQTT service becomes more manageable with multiple brokers. As demand increases, additional brokers can be added to the network to handle increased traffic without significant reconfiguration of existing infrastructure.

Geographic Redundancy:

- Multiple brokers can be strategically located in different geographic regions to reduce latency for clients connecting from various locations and to provide redundancy in case of regional network issues or data center failures.

Architectural Considerations

Designing an MQTT client that can manage connections to multiple brokers involves several key considerations:

Broker Discovery and Selection:

- **Dynamic Broker Discovery**: Implement a mechanism for clients to discover available brokers dynamically. This could be via a central registry that clients check to obtain the addresses of available brokers.
- **Selection Criteria**: Develop criteria for selecting which broker to connect

to, based on factors like current load, geographic proximity, or quality of service requirements.

Connection Management:

- **Handling Failovers**: Clients should be capable of detecting when a broker connection fails and automatically switching to an alternate broker without manual intervention.

Connection Strategies:

- **Random or Round-Robin**: Connect to brokers in a random or round-robin fashion to distribute the load evenly.
- **Priority-Based**: Connect based on predefined priorities assigned to each broker, which could be based on the broker's performance metrics or other operational parameters.

Consistent State Management Across Brokers:

- **Synchronization**: Ensure that client state and session information are consistently maintained across brokers. This might involve replicating client session states or using a centralized store that all brokers can access to retrieve and update state information.
- **Message Integrity**: Ensure that messages are not lost or duplicated when switching between brokers. This might involve transactional messaging or using broker features that support message state synchronization.

Implementing with paho-mqtt in Python:

- Use paho-mqtt's features to manage multiple connections and handle automatic reconnections. Here's a simple example:

Testing and Validation:

- Regularly test the client's ability to handle broker failovers and load distribution effectively. Use simulated environments to emulate broker failures and network disruptions to ensure that the client reacts as expected.

By considering these architectural elements and implementing effective management strategies, MQTT clients can leverage a multi-broker setup to achieve higher levels of reliability, performance, and scalability.

```python
import paho.mqtt.client as mqtt
def on_connect(client, userdata, flags, rc):
    if rc == 0:
        print(f"Connected to {client._host}")
    else:
        print("Failed to connect, attempting next broker")

def connect_to_brokers(brokers):
    for broker in brokers:
        client = mqtt.Client()
        client.on_connect = on_connect
        client.connect(broker, 1883, 60)
        client.loop_start()

brokers = ["broker1.example.com", "broker2.example.com"]
connect_to_brokers(brokers)
```

Testing and Validation:

- Regularly test the client's ability to handle broker failovers and load distribution effectively. Use simulated environments to emulate broker failures and network disruptions to ensure that the client reacts as expected.

By considering these architectural elements and implementing effective management strategies, MQTT clients can leverage a multi-broker setup to achieve higher levels of reliability, performance, and scalability.

Implementing Multi-Broker Connectivity in MQTT Clients

Handling multiple broker connections effectively is crucial for enhancing the robustness and scalability of MQTT applications. This involves not only managing multiple connections but also implementing intelligent load balancing and failover mechanisms. Here's how to adapt your MQTT client to support these capabilities.

Managing Multiple Connections

To manage multiple simultaneous broker connections in an MQTT client, you need to maintain separate client instances for each connection. Each client instance will handle its connection lifecycle, callbacks, and message handling independently.

Example Implementation Using paho-mqtt:

```
import paho.mqtt.client as mqtt

def on_connect(client, udata, flags, rc):
    print(f"Conn to {udata['broker']} with result code {str(rc)}")

def on_message(client, userdata, msg):
    print(f"Rec msg '{str(msg.payload)}' on topic '{msg.topic}'")

# Setup connection for multiple brokers

def setup_multiple_connections(brokers):
    clients = []
    for broker in brokers:
        client = mqtt.Client(userdata={'broker': broker})
        client.on_connect = on_connect
        client.on_message = on_message
        client.connect(broker, 1883, 60)
        client.loop_start()
        clients.append(client)
    return clients

brokers = ["192.168.1.10", "192.168.1.20"]# List of broker IPs
clients = setup_multiple_connections(brokers)
```

In this setup, each MQTT client runs in its thread (managed by paho-mqtt via loop_start()), handling its connection to one of the brokers. This allows for simultaneous operations across multiple brokers.

Load Balancing and Failover

Implementing load balancing and failover involves strategically distributing client connections across available brokers and defining mechanisms to handle broker outages gracefully.

Load Balancing:

- **Round-Robin**: Distribute client connections evenly across the available brokers. This can be achieved by cycling through a list of brokers when initializing client connections.
- **Resource-Based**: Connect to brokers based on current load or response times. This may require a monitoring system to track broker performance metrics in real-time.

Failover:

- **Detecting Disconnections**: Use the on_disconnect callback to detect when a client has lost its connection to a broker.
- **Reconnecting Logic**:

```python
def on_disconnect(client, userdata, rc):
    if rc != 0:
        # Unexpected disconnection
        print(f"disconnection from {userdata['broker']}")
        reconnect_to_broker(client, userdata['broker'])

def reconnect_to_broker(client, broker):
    while True:
        try:
            print(f"Attempting to reconnect to {broker}")
            client.connect(broker, 1883, 60)
            break
        except Exception as e:

print(f"Reconnect failed: {e}")
time.sleep(10) # Wait before retrying
```

Dynamic Broker Selection:

- During the initial connection setup or when handling failures, dynamically select the broker based on predefined criteria (e.g., least connections, best response times).

Broker Health Checks:

- Implement periodic health checks for each broker to evaluate its availability and performance. Adjust the load balancing strategy based on these health checks to avoid directing clients to underperforming or failed brokers.

Best Practices

- **Maintain a Broker Registry**: Keep a dynamic list or registry of active and healthy brokers, updated based on real-time monitoring and health checks.
- **Automate Broker Failover**: Automate the failover process to reduce downtime. Ensure that clients can quickly reconnect to alternate brokers without manual intervention.
- **Testing and Simulation**: Regularly test the load balancing and failover mechanisms under simulated network failures and broker outages to ensure that the system behaves as expected under adverse conditions.

By implementing these strategies, your MQTT client will be better equipped to handle multiple broker connections, distribute load effectively, and manage broker failures gracefully, thus enhancing the overall reliability and efficiency of your MQTT deployment.

Practical Scenarios and Use Cases for Multi-Broker MQTT Connectivity

Implementing multi-broker connectivity in MQTT systems can significantly enhance robustness, scalability, and flexibility across various industries and applications. Here, we explore real-world scenarios where such connectivity is beneficial and present case studies highlighting successful implementations.

Real-World Applications

IoT Device Management:

- **Scenario**: In a large-scale IoT deployment, such as smart city projects involving sensors and devices spread across different geographic locations, connecting to multiple brokers ensures that data routing is efficient and localized, reducing latency and improving response times.

Disaster Recovery:

- **Scenario**: For critical applications like healthcare monitoring systems, having multiple brokers ensures that in the event of a disaster or failure at one site, the system can automatically failover to another broker with minimal disruption, maintaining continuous monitoring and alerting.

Load Distribution in Consumer Applications:

- **Scenario**: Consumer applications, such as messaging platforms or smart home systems, often experience varying loads dynamically. Multiple brokers can distribute this load effectively, ensuring that no single broker becomes a bottleneck, which enhances user experience and system responsiveness.

Global Enterprises:

- **Scenario**: Enterprises operating in multiple regions might use multiple MQTT brokers to handle local traffic effectively. This approach can comply with data residency regulations by ensuring data does not leave a particular region and reducing cross-region data transfer costs.

Case Studies

Smart City Implementation:

- **Overview**: A smart city project implemented a multi-broker MQTT architecture to manage data collection from various sensors (traffic, weather, pollution) distributed throughout the city.
- **Benefit**: By using multiple brokers, the city could manage data more efficiently, ensuring faster processing and response times for critical services like traffic management and emergency responses.
- **Outcome**: The deployment significantly improved the city's ability to monitor and react to urban conditions in real-time, enhancing public safety and environmental monitoring.

Healthcare Monitoring System:

- **Overview**: A healthcare provider implemented an MQTT system with multiple brokers to ensure continuous patient monitoring across various facilities.
- **Benefit**: The multi-broker setup provided redundancy, ensuring that patient data was always available even if one of the brokers failed, crucial for patient care where data availability can directly impact health outcomes.
- **Outcome**: The system's reliability and fault tolerance improved, with healthcare providers able to guarantee round-the-clock monitoring and immediate alerts in critical situations.

International Retail Chain:

- **Overview**: An international retail chain used MQTT brokers located in multiple data centers around the world to manage inventory and customer interactions across its global stores.
- **Benefit**: This setup allowed the company to handle localized data traffic efficiently and comply with international data laws by keeping customer data within its region of origin.
- **Outcome**: The company achieved more accurate inventory management and faster customer service response times, improving overall operational efficiency and compliance with global data privacy regulations.

Best Practices

- **Continuous Monitoring and Testing**: Regularly monitor and test the multi-broker system to ensure that it can handle expected traffic and failover scenarios smoothly.
- **Dynamic Broker Management**: Implement mechanisms to add, remove, or substitute brokers dynamically based on current load and broker performance.
- **Security and Compliance**: Ensure that each broker adheres to the security standards required for the application, especially in regulated industries like healthcare and finance.

By leveraging multiple brokers, organizations can enhance the scalability, reliability, and efficiency of their MQTT deployments, tailoring the architecture to meet specific operational demands and regulatory requirements.

19

Chapter 19: GUI for the MQTT Client Using Tkinter

Introduction to Tkinter

Overview of Tkinter:

Tkinter is the standard GUI (Graphical User Interface) library for Python. It provides a fast and easy way to create simple to complex GUI applications. Tkinter is built into Python, making it widely accessible for anyone to use without the need for installation of any additional packages.

Setup and Configuration:

Setting up a Tkinter window in Python is straightforward. Here's how to create a basic window:

Import Tkinter:

```
import tkinter as tk
```

Create the Main Window:

```
root = tk.Tk()
```

Set the Window Title:

```
root.title("Hello Tkinter")
```

Define Window Size:

```
root.geometry("400x400") # Width x Height
```

Start the Main Event Loop:

```
root.mainloop()
```

This loop is essential as it keeps the window active and waits for the user to perform an action.

With these simple steps, you have a basic Tkinter window up and running, ready for adding more widgets and functionalities.

Designing the GUI for an MQTT Client Using Tkinter

Designing a user-friendly GUI for an MQTT client involves careful planning of the layout and judicious selection of widgets to provide an intuitive and functional interface. Here's a guide on how to approach the layout planning and widget selection for your MQTT client.

Layout Planning

Define Functional Requirements:

- Before you start designing the GUI, clearly define what functionalities your MQTT client needs to support. Common functions include connecting to a broker, subscribing to topics, publishing messages, and displaying incoming messages.

Sketch the Interface:

- Use a simple sketch or wireframe to layout the placement of controls like buttons, text fields, and display areas. This helps in visualizing the user interface and planning the functional grouping of widgets.

Use Frames for Organization:

- Utilize tk.Frame widgets to logically group related elements in your GUI. For example, use one frame for connection settings, another for publish controls, and another for subscription settings.

Responsive Design:

- Consider making your layout responsive by using grid geometry manager, which allows your application to adjust gracefully to different window sizes. Avoid using the pack manager for complex layouts as it offers less precision.

Widget Selection

Buttons:

- **Usage**: Use buttons for actions like "Connect", "Disconnect", "Subscribe", and "Publish".

Code Example:

```
connect_button = tk.Button(
                        root,
                        text="Connect",
                        command=connect_to_broker
                        )

connect_button.grid(row=0, column=0, padx=10, pady=10)
```

Text Entries:

Usage: Text entry widgets are essential for inputs like the broker address, port number, topic name, and the payload for messages.

Code Example:

```
broker_address = tk.Entry(root)
broker_address.grid(row=1, column=1, padx=10, pady=10)
```

Labels:

Usage: Use labels to identify different input fields, status messages, or to simply display text such as instructions.

Code Example:

```
label = tk.Label(root, text="Broker Address:")
label.grid(row=1, column=0, padx=10, pady=10)
```

Message Boxes:

Usage: Message boxes are useful for notifications like successful connection, errors, and other alerts.

Code Example:

```
import tkinter.messagebox as messagebox
messagebox.showinfo(
                "Success",
                "Successfully connected to the broker."
                )
```

Scrollable Text Area:

Usage: A text area, possibly with a scrollbar, is necessary for displaying incoming messages or logs.

Code Example:

```
from tkinter import scrolledtext
log_area = scrolledtext.ScrolledText(
                                    root,
                                    width=40,
                                    height=10
                        )
log_area.grid(
            row=3,
            column=0,
            columnspan=2,
            padx=10,
            pady=10
            )
```

Finalizing the Design

- **Consistency**: Ensure that the GUI design is consistent in terms of fonts, button sizes, and color schemes, which aids in user familiarity and accessibility.
- **Feedback Loops**: Implement visual or textual feedback for every user interaction to indicate the state of the system (e.g., connected, disconnected).
- **Testing**: Test the GUI with potential end-users for usability. Gather feedback and make necessary adjustments to improve the interface.

By following these guidelines, you can create an effective and user-friendly GUI for your MQTT client that enhances the interaction experience and functionality.

Implementing MQTT Operations in the GUI using Tkinter

Creating an interactive GUI for managing MQTT operations like connecting to a broker, publishing messages, and subscribing to topics can greatly enhance the usability of your MQTT client. Here's how to integrate these functionalities into your Tkinter GUI.

Connecting to a Broker

GUI Elements:

- Create input fields for the broker's address and port, and buttons for "Connect" and "Disconnect".

Example:

```python
import tkinter as tk
import paho.mqtt.client as mqtt

def connect_broker():
    broker_address = broker_entry.get()
    port = int(port_entry.get())
    client.connect(broker_address, port=port)
    client.loop_start()

def disconnect_broker():
    client.disconnect()
```

Connecting to a Broker Part A

```
root = tk.Tk()
root.title("MQTT Client")

tk.Label(
        root,
        text="Broker Address:").grid(row=0, column=0
        )
broker_entry = tk.Entry(root)
broker_entry.grid(row=0, column=1)

tk.Label(root, text="Port:").grid(row=1, column=0)
    port_entry = tk.Entry(root)
    port_entry.grid(row=1, column=1)
```

Connecting to a Broker Part B

```
connect_button = tk.Button(
                        root,
                        text="Connect",
                        command=connect_broker
                        )
connect_button.grid(row=2, column=0)

disconnect_button = tk.Button(
                        root,
                        text="Disconnect",
                        command=disconnect_broker
                        )
 disconnect_button.grid(row=2, column=1) client = mqtt.Client()
```

Connecting to a Broker Part C

Publishing and Subscribing

Publishing Messages:

Add input fields for the topic and the message payload along with a "Publish" button.

Example:

```
def publish_message():
    topic = topic_entry.get()
    message = message_entry.get()
    client.publish(topic, message)

tk.Label(root, text="Publish Topic:").grid(row=3, column=0)
    topic_entry = tk.Entry(root) topic_entry.grid(
                                        row=3,
                                        column=1
                                        )

tk.Label(root, text="Message:").grid(row=4, column=0)
    message_entry = tk.Entry(root)
    message_entry.grid(row=4, column=1)

publish_button = tk.Button(
                        root,
                        text="Publish",
                        command=publish_message
                        )

publish_button.grid(row=5, column=1)
```

Subscribing to Topics:

Implement functionality to allow users to subscribe to topics.

Example:

```
def subscribe_topic():
    topic = subscribe_entry.get()
    client.subscribe(topic)

tk.Label(root, text="Subscribe Topic:").grid(row=6, column=0)
    subscribe_entry = tk.Entry(root)
    subscribe_entry.grid(row=6, column=1)

subscribe_button = tk.Button(
                        root,
                        text="Subscribe",
                        command=subscribe_topic
                    )

subscribe_button.grid(row=7, column=1)
```

Displaying Messages

Incoming Messages:

Use a text area to display incoming messages. A ScrolledText widget can be useful here for scrollable message logs.

Example:

```
from tkinter import scrolledtext

def on_message(client, userdata, message):
    message_display.insert(
                        tk.END,
                        f"{message.topic}:
                        {message.payload.decode()}\n"
                        )

client.on_message = on_message
message_display = scrolledtext.ScrolledText(root, height=10)
message_display.grid(row=8, column=0, columnspan=2)

root.mainloop()
```

These snippets collectively demonstrate how to integrate MQTT operations within a Tkinter-based GUI, enhancing the interactivity and functionality of your MQTT client. Each component is designed to interact seamlessly, providing a comprehensive interface for users to manage MQTT connections and communications effectively.

Enhancing Usability and Functionality in MQTT Client GUI

To elevate the user experience and functional prowess of your MQTT client GUI, incorporating clear user feedback, robust error handling, and advanced features is essential. Here's how to effectively enhance your MQTT GUI using Tkinter.

User Feedback and Error Handling

Connection Status:

- Display real-time connection status updates to inform the user whether they are connected, attempting to connect, or disconnected.

Example:

```
status_label = tk.Label(root, text="Disconnected", fg="red")
status_label.grid(row=9, column=0, columnspan=2)

def update_status(message, color):
    status_label.config(text=message, fg=color)

def on_connect(client, userdata, flags, rc):
    if rc == 0:
        update_status("Connected", "green")
    else:
        update_status(
                        f"Failed to connect,
                        return code {rc}",
                        "red"
                     )

def on_disconnect(client, userdata, rc):
    update_status("Disconnected", "red")
```

Publishing Feedback:

Provide visual or textual feedback when messages are successfully published or if there is a failure.

Example:

```
def publish_message():
  try:
    topic = topic_entry.get()
    message = message_entry.get()
    client.publish(topic, message)
    update_status("Message published successfully", "blue")
  except Exception as e:
    update_status(f"Publish failed: {str(e)}", "red")
```

Error Notifications:

Use message boxes or status labels to display error messages for various operations like failed connections, publish errors, or subscription issues.

Example:

```
import tkinter.messagebox as messagebox

def on_publish(client, userdata, mid):
  messagebox.showinfo(
                "Publish Success",
                "Message published successfully!"
                )

client.on_publish = on_publish
```

Advanced Features

Logging:

Implement a logging system to record all actions, events, and errors. Display these logs in a part of your GUI to help with debugging and monitoring.

Example:

```
from tkinter import scrolledtext

log_area = scrolledtext.ScrolledText(root, height=10)
log_area.grid(row=10, column=0, columnspan=2)

def log(message):
    log_area.insert(tk.END, f"{message}\n")
    log_area.yview(tk.END)
```

Topic Subscription Management:

Provide a dynamic interface for managing subscriptions, allowing users to add, remove, or modify their topic subscriptions.

Example:

```
def unsubscribe_topic():
    topic = subscribe_entry.get()
    client.unsubscribe(topic)
    log("Unsubscribed from " + topic)

unsubscribe_button = tk.Button(
                            root,
                            text="Unsubscribe",
                            command=unsubscribe_topic
                        )

unsubscribe_button.grid(row=7, column=2)
```

Client Settings Customization:

· Allow users to customize settings such as MQTT version, keep alive intervals, and clean sessions via the GUI.

Example:

```
settings_frame = tk.LabelFrame(
                                root,
                                text="Settings",
                                padx=10,
                                pady=10
                        )
settings_frame.grid(
                        padx=10,
                        pady=10,
                        row=11,
                        column=0,
                        columnspan=2
                )
clean_session_var = tk.BooleanVar(value=True)
tk.Checkbutton(
                settings_frame,
                text="Clean Session",
                variable=clean_session_var
                ).pack(anchor='w')
tk.Label(settings_frame, text="Keep Alive:").pack(anchor='w')
keep_alive_entry = tk.Entry(settings_frame)
keep_alive_entry.pack()
```

By implementing these enhancements, your MQTT client GUI will not only provide a richer and more interactive user experience but also equip users with powerful tools and functionalities for effective communication and debugging. These improvements make the client more robust, versatile, and user-friendly, catering to both novice users and experienced professionals.

20

Chapter 20: Introduction to MQTT Security

The Importance of Security in MQTT

MQTT (Message Queuing Telemetry Transport) is a lightweight messaging protocol widely used in IoT (Internet of Things) applications for its efficiency and low bandwidth usage. However, the simplicity and widespread use of MQTT also bring several security challenges and vulnerabilities that must be addressed to protect the data and integrity of MQTT-based systems.

Security Challenges in MQTT

Lightweight Protocol with Limited Built-in Security:

- MQTT was originally designed for trusted networks with minimal security features. The protocol itself does not include advanced security mechanisms, making it inherently vulnerable when exposed to untrusted environments like the internet.

Large-Scale Deployment:

- The widespread use of MQTT in large-scale IoT applications increases the attack surface. With thousands, if not millions, of devices connected, ensuring consistent security across all devices becomes challenging.

Resource-Constrained Devices:

- Many MQTT clients run on resource-constrained devices that may lack the computational power necessary for complex security measures, such as SSL/TLS encryption.

Broker Reliability:

- As the central point of message routing, MQTT brokers are critical components that, if compromised, can disrupt the entire communication network.

Common Security Threats in MQTT Implementations

Eavesdropping:

- **Description**: Intercepting messages between clients and brokers to gain unauthorized access to sensitive information.
- **Impact**: Compromises the confidentiality of data transmitted over the network, potentially revealing sensitive information about system operations or user data.

Unauthorized Access:

- **Description**: Gaining unauthorized access to the MQTT broker or client to publish or subscribe to topics illegitimately.
- **Impact**: Leads to data breaches, where attackers can both retrieve

sensitive information and send malicious commands to control devices.

Data Tampering:

- **Description**: Modifying messages in transit between clients and brokers.
- **Impact**: Can lead to harmful actions being taken by IoT devices, based on the tampered data, potentially causing physical and operational damage.

Denial of Service (DoS):

- **Description**: Flooding the broker with a high volume of messages or malformed packets to overwhelm the system.
- **Impact**: Can render the service unavailable, disrupting legitimate use and potentially causing system outages.

Man-in-the-Middle Attacks:

- **Description**: Intercepting and altering communications between two parties without their knowledge.
- **Impact**: Allows attackers to steal or manipulate data by impersonating the client or broker, leading to loss of integrity and trust in the system.

Mitigation Strategies

To address these security issues, robust security measures are essential:

Encryption:

- Implement SSL/TLS encryption for all communications between MQTT clients and brokers to protect data in transit from eavesdropping and tampering.

Authentication and Authorization:

- Use strong authentication mechanisms to ensure that only authorized clients can connect to the broker. Consider using certificate-based authentication, which offers higher security than traditional username and password.
- Implement fine-grained access control policies to restrict who can publish or subscribe to specific topics, mitigating the risk of unauthorized access.

Regular Security Audits and Updates:

- Conduct regular security audits to identify and address vulnerabilities.
- Ensure that all components of the MQTT system, including clients, brokers, and libraries, are regularly updated to the latest versions containing security patches.

Secure Configuration:

- Harden MQTT configurations to avoid common misconfigurations, such as disabling unused features, securing default settings, and ensuring that all network interfaces of the MQTT broker are secured.

Network Security:

- Implement network security measures such as firewalls, intrusion detection systems (IDS), and virtual private networks (VPNs) to provide additional layers of security.

By understanding and addressing these security challenges and threats, organizations can significantly enhance the security posture of their MQTT-based systems, protecting them against potential attacks and ensuring the safe and reliable operation of their IoT devices and applications.

Basic Security Mechanisms for MQTT

Ensuring the security of MQTT communications is crucial for protecting data integrity and privacy in IoT and other networked applications. Implementing foundational security mechanisms such as TLS/SSL for transport security, basic authentication methods, and payload encryption can significantly enhance the overall security of MQTT systems.

Using MQTT Over TLS/SSL

Introduction to TLS/SSL:

- **Transport Layer Security (TLS)** and its predecessor, Secure Sockets Layer (SSL), are cryptographic protocols designed to provide secure communication over a computer network. When applied to MQTT, TLS/SSL ensures that the data transferred between the MQTT client and the broker is encrypted, thus providing confidentiality and integrity of messages.

Benefits:

- **Eavesdropping Prevention**: TLS/SSL encrypts the data being transmitted, preventing unauthorized parties from reading the messages.
- **Tampering Prevention**: TLS/SSL includes mechanisms to verify that the data has not been altered in transit, safeguarding against tampering.

Implementation:

- Configuring MQTT to use TLS/SSL typically involves setting up the MQTT broker to accept secure connections and configuring the client to use TLS/SSL when connecting:

```
import paho.mqtt.client as mqtt

def on_connect(client, userdata, flags, rc):
    if rc == 0:
        print("Connected successfully.")
    else:
        print("Connection failed.")

client = mqtt.Client()
client.on_connect = on_connect

client.tls_set(
            ca_certs="path/to/ca.crt",
            certfile="path/to/client.crt",
            keyfile="path/to/client.key",
            tls_version=mqtt.ssl.PROTOCOL_TLSv1_2
            ) client.connect("mqtt.example.com", 8883, 60)
# Note the use of port 8883 for TLS/SSL connections
client.loop_forever()
```

Authentication Methods

Basic Authentication:

Basic authentication using usernames and passwords is the simplest form of authenticating MQTT clients to ensure that only authorized users can connect to the MQTT broker.

Setup:

Broker Configuration: Configure the MQTT broker to require username and password authentication.

- **Client Configuration**: Modify the MQTT client to provide the username and password upon connection:

```
client.username_pw_set("username", "password")
```

Security Considerations:

- While convenient, username and password authentication can be vulnerable if not used in conjunction with TLS/SSL, as credentials could be intercepted by attackers. Always use TLS/SSL when transmitting sensitive information like passwords.

Encryption of Payloads

Payload Encryption:

- Encrypting message payloads provides an additional layer of security, ensuring that sensitive data remains confidential, even if an attacker bypasses other security measures.

Importance:

- In environments where highly sensitive data is transmitted, or where additional security is required, payload encryption protects data beyond the built-in capabilities of MQTT and TLS/SSL.

Implementation:

- Use encryption libraries to encrypt the payload before publishing and decrypt upon receiving. Common libraries for Python include py-cryptodome:

```python
from Crypto.Cipher import AES
import base64

# Encryption
def encrypt_message(message, key):
    cipher = AES.new(
                    key,
                    AES.MODE_EAX
                    )
nonce = cipher.nonce
ciphertext, tag = cipher.encrypt_and_digest(
                                    Message.encode('utf-8')
                                    )
return base64.b64encode(
                        nonce + tag + ciphertext
                        ).decode('utf-8')
```

Implementation Part A

```
# Decryption
def decrypt_message(enc_message, key):
    enc_message_bytes = base64.b64decode(enc_message)
    nonce = enc_message_bytes[:16]
    tag = enc_message_bytes[16:32]
    ciphertext = enc_message_bytes[32:]
    cipher = AES.new(key, AES.MODE_EAX, nonce=nonce)
    decrypted_message = cipher.decrypt_and_verify(
                                                ciphertext,
                                                tag
                                                )
    return decrypted_message.decode('utf-8')
```

Implementation Part B

Best Practices:

- **Key Management**: Manage encryption keys securely using a key management system (KMS). Rotate keys periodically to limit the exposure
  of encrypted data to a single key.
- **Comprehensive Security**: Combine payload encryption with TLS/SSL
  and robust authentication to provide multiple layers of security.

Implementing these basic security mechanisms provides a solid foundation
for securing MQTT communications against common threats, ensuring the
confidentiality, integrity, and availability of the transmitted data.

Best Practices for MQTT Security

Ensuring robust security in MQTT implementations involves not only
employing strong security measures but also maintaining vigilant and
consistent management practices. Here are detailed best practices for

securely configuring MQTT brokers and clients, as well as the necessity of conducting regular security audits and updates.

Security Configuration Tips

Use TLS/SSL for All Connections:

- **Implementation**: Configure both the MQTT broker and clients to use TLS/SSL connections to encrypt all data in transit, preventing eavesdropping and tampering. Always use certificates from a trusted Certificate Authority (CA).

Enable Strong Authentication:

- **Methods**: Beyond basic username and password authentication, implement stronger mechanisms like mutual TLS (mTLS), where both the client and the broker authenticate each other using certificates.
- **Two-Factor Authentication**: For critical applications, consider implementing two-factor authentication for administrative access to the broker.

Implement Authorization with Fine-Grained Control:

- **Access Control Lists (ACLs)**: Define ACLs to specify which topics a client can publish to and subscribe from. This limits the ability of any compromised client to interact outside its designated parameters.
- **Role-Based Access Control (RBAC)**: Use RBAC to define roles for different types of clients and assign permissions based on these roles.

Use Secure Configuration Settings:

- **Disable Unused Features**: Turn off any non-essential features or services running on the MQTT broker to minimize the attack surface.
- **Configure Keep Alive and Timeout Settings**: Properly configure session timeouts and keep-alive intervals to drop inactive or potentially rogue connections.
- **Logging and Monitoring**: Enable detailed logging of connections, disconnections, and messaging activities. Use these logs to monitor for unusual activities that might indicate an attack.

Network Segmentation and Firewalling:

- **Segmentation**: Use network segmentation to isolate the MQTT broker from the rest of the network. This limits the potential for lateral movement in case of a network breach.
- **Firewall Rules**: Implement strict firewall rules to control which devices can communicate with the MQTT broker, restricting access to trusted devices only.

Regular Security Audits and Updates

Conduct Regular Security Audits:

- **Purpose**: Regular audits help identify vulnerabilities, misconfigurations, and compliance issues that could compromise the security of the MQTT environment.
- **Components**: Audits should cover network security, application security, and even physical security aspects related to the MQTT deployment.
- **Penetration Testing**: Periodically engage in penetration testing to actively exploit vulnerabilities, helping to understand the real-world risks associated with current security configurations.

Regular Updates and Patch Management:

- **Broker and Client Software**: Keep the MQTT broker and client software up-to-date with the latest security patches. This protects against known vulnerabilities that could be exploited by attackers.
- **Operating System and Dependencies**: Regularly update the operating systems and any dependencies used by MQTT brokers and clients to mitigate security risks from outdated software.

Continuous Improvement:

- **Feedback Loop**: Use the insights gained from monitoring and audits to continually refine and improve security policies and controls.
- **Security Training**: Ensure that all personnel involved in managing and developing MQTT systems are trained in security best practices and are aware of the latest security threats.

By adhering to these best practices for MQTT security, organizations can significantly enhance the protection of their MQTT environments against common and sophisticated security threats. Regular audits and proactive security management are essential to maintaining the integrity and confidentiality of MQTT communications.

21

Chapter 21: Implementing SSL/TLS in MQTT

SSL/TLS Basics

Secure Sockets Layer (SSL) and its successor, Transport Layer Security (TLS), are fundamental to securing communications over computer networks. Understanding how these protocols work and their benefits is crucial for implementing robust security measures in any networked environment.

Overview of SSL/TLS

SSL/TLS operates between the transport layer and the application layer in the network stack, effectively encapsulating the data of higher-level protocols like HTTP, FTP, and SMTP. Here's a basic outline of how SSL/TLS works:

Connection Establishment:

- **Handshake Process**: The SSL/TLS handshake initiates when a client and server start a session. This process establishes the cryptographic parameters of the session, including the following key steps:

- **Protocol Version Negotiation**: The client and server agree on the SSL/TLS version to use.
- **Cipher Suite Negotiation**: They also agree on the cipher suite, which determines the encryption algorithm and key exchange method.
- **Authentication and Key Exchange**: The server (and optionally the client) authenticates itself using digital certificates. Key exchange allows both parties to establish a shared secret key.

Transmission of Data:

- Once the secure connection is established, data transmission begins. Data is encrypted and decrypted using the agreed-upon encryption algorithms and keys.
- **Session Keys**: These are symmetric keys used for encrypting data transmitted during an SSL/TLS session. They are derived during the handshake phase.

Data Integrity and Confidentiality:

- **Encryption**: Ensures that data cannot be read or tampered with by unauthorized parties.
- **MAC (Message Authentication Code)**: Each message transmitted includes a MAC, which uses a hash function and a secret key to ensure the message's integrity.

Benefits of SSL/TLS

End-to-End Encryption:

- **Data Privacy**: SSL/TLS ensures that data transmitted between the client and server is encrypted, protecting sensitive information from eavesdroppers.
- **Example**: When you visit an HTTPS website, the data exchanged between

your browser and the server is encrypted with SSL/TLS, making it unreadable to anyone who might intercept the transmission.

Authentication:

- **Verifying Identities**: The use of SSL/TLS certificates helps verify the identity of the parties. When a server presents its certificate to a client, the client can verify that the certificate is valid and issued by a trusted Certificate Authority (CA).
- **Trust Establishment**: This authentication process helps establish trust, ensuring that clients are indeed communicating with the intended server and not an imposter.

Data Integrity:

- **Protection Against Tampering**: The integrity of data is maintained through the use of hash functions and MACs. This ensures that any alterations to the transmitted data can be detected by the receiving end.

Non-Repudiation:

- **Assurance of Origin**: By using digital signatures, SSL/TLS provides assurances that a message or transaction has indeed originated from a specific party. This is crucial for scenarios where proof of origin is required for legal or verification purposes.

Secure Key Exchange:

- **Safe Sharing of Keys**: SSL/TLS provides mechanisms like Diffie-Hellman or RSA-based key exchanges that allow secure sharing of keys even over an insecure channel. This enables both parties to encrypt and decrypt messages securely without exposing their secret keys.

Understanding and leveraging the security capabilities of SSL/TLS is essential for any application that communicates over potentially insecure networks. By ensuring confidentiality, integrity, and authentication, SSL/TLS plays a pivotal role in safeguarding data and maintaining trust in the digital world.

Configuring SSL/TLS for MQTT

Implementing SSL/TLS in MQTT communications enhances the security by ensuring that the data transmitted between the MQTT clients and broker is encrypted and authenticated. Here's how to manage SSL certificates and configure both MQTT brokers and clients to use SSL/TLS.

Certificate Management

Obtaining SSL Certificates:

- **Certificate Authority (CA)**: The most secure way to obtain an SSL certificate is through a recognized Certificate Authority (CA) like Let's Encrypt, Comodo, or DigiCert. These certificates are trusted by most software out of the box.
- **Generate Self-Signed Certificates**: For development or private networks, you can create self-signed certificates. Here's how to do it using OpenSSL:

```
# Generate a private key
openssl genrsa -out ca.key 2048

# Generate a certificate signing request (CSR)
openssl req -new -key ca.key -out ca.csr

# Generate a self-signed certificate
openssl x509 -req -days 365 -in ca.csr -signkey ca.key -out ca.crt
```

Managing Certificates:

- **Storage**: Store certificates and keys securely. Ensure access is limited to only those processes that require them.
- **Renewal and Revocation:** Track the expiry dates of your certificates and renew them before they expire. Set up mechanisms to revoke certificates if they are compromised.
- **Broker Configuration:** Setting Up SSL/TLS on MQTT Broker (Mosquitto)

Configuration Steps:

Place your CA certificate (ca.crt), server certificate (server.crt), and server key (server.key) in the Mosquitto configuration directory.

- Edit the Mosquitto configuration file (mosquitto.conf) to enable SSL/TLS:

```
listener 8883 cafile /path/to/ca.crt
certfile /path/to/server.crt
keyfile /path/to/server.key
```

- **Note**: listener 8883 tells Mosquitto to listen on port 8883, which is commonly used for encrypted MQTT traffic.

Restart the Broker:

- Restart the Mosquitto broker to apply the new configuration.

```
sudo systemctl restart mosquitto
```

Client Configuration: Connecting Clients Securely

MQTT Client Setup:

Clients must also be configured to trust the CA that issued the broker's certificate. If using a self-signed certificate, the client needs to explicitly trust it.

- **Example Configuration using Paho MQTT Python**:

```
import paho.mqtt.client as mqtt

def on_connect(client, userdata, flags, rc):
    if rc == 0:
        print("Connected with result code " + str(rc))
    else:
        print(
            "Failed to connect,
            return code " + str(rc)
            )

client = mqtt.Client()
client.on_connect = on_connect client.tls_set(
                    ca_certs="/path/to/ca.crt",
                    tls_version=mqtt.ssl.PROTOCOL_TLSv1_2
                    )
client.connect("mqtt.example.com", 8883, 60)
# Note the port number here is 8883 for SSL/TLS
client.loop_forever()
```

- **Client Certificate Authentication**: If you require clients to also authenticate using certificates:

```
client.tls_set(
                ca_certs="/path/to/ca.crt",
                certfile="/path/to/client.crt",
                keyfile="/path/to/client.key",
                tls_version=mqtt.ssl.PROTOCOL_TLSv1_2
                )
```

Best Practices

- **Regularly Update Your SSL/TLS Configuration**: Stay updated with the latest in security practices and update your TLS settings to disable older, vulnerable protocols or ciphers.
- **Monitor and Log**: Keep detailed logs of SSL/TLS handshake failures and regularly monitor these logs for any signs of malicious activity or misconfiguration.

By following these guidelines, you can ensure that your MQTT communication is secure, helping to protect your data from eavesdropping and tampering.

Testing and Troubleshooting SSL/TLS Implementations

Ensuring that SSL/TLS configurations are properly set up and functioning correctly is crucial for maintaining the security of network communications. Here are methods and tools for verification, as well as common issues and their resolutions.

Verification Tools

OpenSSL:

- **OpenSSL** is a powerful tool to manually check, verify, and debug SSL/TLS configurations on servers.
- **Example Command to Test SSL Connection**:

```
openssl s_client -connect servername:port -CAfile ca.crt
```

This command allows you to initiate a connection to an MQTT broker using SSL and provides detailed output of the SSL handshake process, including the certificate chain and any errors encountered.

SSL Labs' SSL Test:

- For internet-facing servers, **SSL Labs' SSL Test** offers a comprehensive online tool to check the strength of SSL/TLS settings on public IP addresses. It provides a thorough report that includes ratings and recommendations.

Wireshark:

- **Wireshark** can capture network packets and is particularly useful for analyzing the SSL/TLS handshake process and identifying problems with encryption settings or certificate exchanges.

MQTT.fx / MQTT Explorer:

- GUI-based MQTT clients like **MQTT.fx** and **MQTT Explorer** can connect to your broker using SSL/TLS and will report connection issues related to SSL/TLS, helping to troubleshoot client-side configurations.

Common SSL/TLS Issues and Resolutions

Certificate Not Trusted:

- **Issue**: If the certificate chain is incomplete or if the CA is not trusted, clients will fail to establish a secure connection.
- **Resolution**: Ensure that all necessary intermediate certificates are included in the server's certificate file. On the client side, ensure that the CA certificate used to sign the broker's certificate is included in the client's trust store.

Protocol or Cipher Mismatch:

- **Issue**: Clients and servers must agree on the protocol and cipher to use. Mismatches can prevent successful connections.
- **Resolution**: Check the server's configuration to ensure that it supports the protocols and ciphers that the clients use. Tools like **openssl s_client** can help identify which ciphers and SSL/TLS versions are supported by the server.

Expired Certificates:

- **Issue**: SSL/TLS certificates have a validity period, and using an expired certificate will result in a failed connection.
- **Resolution**: Regularly check certificate expiration dates and renew certificates well before they expire. Automate alerts for upcoming expirations as a proactive measure.

Incorrect Server Name:

- **Issue**: The server name in the client's request must match the Common Name (CN) or one of the Subject Alternative Names (SANs) in the server's certificate.
- **Resolution**: Verify the server name in the certificate. If using virtual hosts, ensure that each host's certificate correctly lists the expected

server name.

Port and Firewall Issues:

- **Issue**: Incorrect port configurations or firewall rules blocking SSL/TLS ports can prevent connections.
- **Resolution**: Ensure that the correct port (commonly 8883 for MQTT over SSL) is open on the server and that no firewall rules are blocking these connections.

Logging and Detailed Errors:

- **Enhancement**: Enable detailed logging on both the MQTT broker and client. Many SSL/TLS libraries offer options to log detailed diagnostic information which can be invaluable for troubleshooting.

By employing these tools and being aware of common SSL/TLS issues, you can effectively verify, test, and troubleshoot your MQTT SSL/TLS implementations, ensuring secure and reliable encrypted communications.

22

Chapter 22: Using Access Control Lists (ACLs) in MQTT

Introduction to Access Control Lists (ACLs) in MQTT

Access Control Lists (ACLs) are a crucial security mechanism used in network communications, including MQTT, to manage permissions and secure data access. ACLs help ensure that only authorized clients can publish to or subscribe from specific MQTT topics, thereby enhancing the overall security of the MQTT broker.

Purpose of ACLs

Managing Permissions:

- ACLs define which clients have permissions to access specific resources. In the context of MQTT, these resources are the topics on which messages are published and subscribed. By controlling access to these topics, ACLs help prevent unauthorized access and ensure that clients only receive data they are permitted to see.

Enhancing Security:

- ACLs help secure MQTT brokers by explicitly defining who can publish or subscribe to certain topics, reducing the risk of malicious or accidental misuse of the MQTT broker. This is particularly important in environments where multiple users or devices interact with the same MQTT broker and where data sensitivity varies.

Regulatory Compliance:

- In many industries, regulations require that data access be controlled and logged. ACLs not only enforce these access policies but also provide an audit trail that can be used to demonstrate compliance with regulatory standards.

How ACLs Work

1. **Topic-Based Permissions**:

- ACLs operate on a per-topic basis. Each entry in an ACL specifies the actions (publish, subscribe) that a client is allowed to perform on a given topic. This allows for granular control over client interactions with the MQTT broker.

Setting Up ACLs:

- In MQTT, ACLs are typically configured on the broker. The broker uses these lists to check each client request against the ACLs to determine if the action should be allowed.

Example of ACL Configuration:

- Consider a scenario where you have two types of clients: sensors and controllers. Sensors publish to topics like sensor/data, and controllers subscribe to sensor/data and publish to control/actuate.
- An ACL might look like this:
- Sensors can publish to sensor/data.
- Controllers can subscribe to sensor/data and publish to control/actuate.

Wildcards and ACLs:

- MQTT supports the use of wildcards (+ for single-level, # for multi-level) in topic subscriptions, and these can also be incorporated into ACLs. This allows for more flexible permissions settings.

Example:

- An ACL entry that allows a client to subscribe to all subtopics under sensor/ could be set as sensor/#. This means the client can subscribe to sensor/data, sensor/status, etc., but not to topics outside of the sensor/ hierarchy.

Implementing ACLs in Common MQTT Brokers:

- **Mosquitto**: Mosquitto supports ACLs through a configuration file (mosquitto.conf) where each line specifies a user and the topic patterns they can access.
- **EMQ X**: EMQ X provides a similar mechanism but also offers a more dynamic ACL configuration via its dashboard or API, allowing for real-time updates to ACLs without restarting the broker.

Best Practices for Using ACLs

- **Principle of Least Privilege**: Always configure ACLs to give clients the minimum level of access necessary for their function. This limits potential damage in case of compromised credentials.
- **Regular Audits**: Regularly review and audit ACL settings to ensure they still reflect current needs and security policies.
- **Secure Management**: Treat ACL configurations as sensitive data. Ensure that only authorized personnel can view or modify ACL settings.

By effectively using ACLs, organizations can significantly enhance the security of their MQTT environments, ensuring that clients can only access topics they are explicitly authorized to access, thus maintaining the integrity and confidentiality of the data transmitted via MQTT.

Implementing ACLs in MQTT

Access Control Lists (ACLs) play a crucial role in securing MQTT brokers by specifying which users can access specific topics. Effective implementation of ACLs involves careful planning and precise configuration. Below, we outline steps for designing ACL policies and configuring them on MQTT brokers.

Designing ACL Policies

Defining User Roles and Permissions:

- **Identify User Types**: Start by identifying different types of users or clients that will interact with your MQTT broker. For example, in a smart home setup, you might have sensor nodes, control devices, and administrative interfaces.
- **Define Roles**: Assign roles based on user types. Roles might include publishers, subscribers, or admin.

Specify Permissions for Each Role:

- **Publishers** might have permission to publish to specific topics like home/sensors/+.
- **Subscribers** might only subscribe to topics like home/alarms/#.
- **Admin** might have unrestricted access to all topics for management purposes.
- **Example Role Definitions**:

```
Role: Sensor
Permissions: Publish to home/sensors/+

Role: User Device
Permissions: Subscribe to home/controls/+

Role: Administrator
Permissions: Publish and Subscribe to all topics
```

Configuring ACLs on the Broker

ACL Configuration Examples:

The configuration of ACLs can vary depending on the MQTT broker being used. Below are examples for configuring ACLs in Mosquitto, a popular MQTT broker.

Mosquitto ACL Configuration:

ACL File Setup:

- Mosquitto uses a plain text file for ACL definitions. Here's how you can structure this file:

```
# Allow anonymous users to read public topics
user anonymous
topic read public/#

# Define permissions for sensor nodes
user sensor1
topic write home/sensors/temperature
topic write home/sensors/humidity

# User device permissions
user userdevice1
topic read home/controls/light
topic read home/controls/temperature

# Admin user permissions
user admin
topic readwrite #
```

Integrating the ACL File with Mosquitto:

- Include the ACL file in your mosquitto.conf:

```
acl_file /etc/mosquitto/aclfile.acl
```

Reload or Restart Mosquitto:

- After updating the ACL file and configuration, reload the Mosquitto configuration or restart the Mosquitto service:

```
sudo systemctl restart mosquitto
```

Best Practices for Implementing ACLs

- **Use Specific Topic Naming Conventions**: Design your topic hierarchy to make it easier to assign and manage ACLs. This includes using clear and distinct base topics for different user groups or device types.
- **Regularly Update ACLs**: As new clients are added or roles change, regularly update your ACLs to reflect these changes. This ensures ongoing security and relevance of permissions.
- **Audit and Log ACL Decisions**: Enable logging in your MQTT broker to track ACL decisions. This can help in troubleshooting access issues and auditing security compliance.
- **Secure ACL Files**: Keep your ACL files secure and backed up. Restrict access to these files to prevent unauthorized modifications.

By carefully designing and implementing ACL policies, you can significantly enhance the security of your MQTT infrastructure, ensuring that only authorized clients can publish or subscribe to specific topics, thereby protecting your networked resources.

Best Practices for Managing ACLs

Effective management of Access Control Lists (ACLs) is vital for maintaining the security integrity of any MQTT deployment. As your system evolves and scales, it's essential to manage ACLs meticulously to avoid security vulnerabilities. Here are best practices for maintaining ACLs and understanding their security implications.

Maintaining ACLs

Regular Updates and Reviews:

- **Routine Audits**: Conduct regular audits of ACL settings to ensure they align with current security policies and operational requirements. This is especially important in dynamic environments where devices or users are frequently added or removed.
- **Update Procedures**: Establish clear procedures for updating ACLs. This should include who is authorized to make changes and under what circumstances changes can be made.

Scalability Considerations:

- **Automated Tools**: As the system scales, manually updating ACLs may become untenable. Consider implementing automated tools or scripts that can manage ACL changes more efficiently.
- **Group-Based Management**: Use group-based ACL management where possible. Managing permissions based on groups rather than individual user entries can simplify administration as the number of clients grows.

Version Control:

- **Backup and Versioning**: Keep versions of your ACL files in a version control system. This not only provides backups but also allows you to easily revert to previous configurations if an error is made or if an update introduces issues.

Security Implications of ACLs

Risks of Misconfiguration:

- **Overly Permissive ACLs**: One of the most common pitfalls is configuring ACLs that are too permissive, potentially allowing unauthorized access to sensitive topics. Always adhere to the principle of least privilege, granting only the minimum necessary permissions for a client to function.
- **Under-restrictive ACLs**: Conversely, overly restrictive ACLs can hinder legitimate operations and lead to operational inefficiencies, prompting users to find workarounds that may compromise security.

Security Best Practices:

- **Explicit Deny**: Where possible, configure ACLs to deny all permissions by default and explicitly allow only specific actions. This approach minimizes the chances of inadvertently granting excessive permissions.
- **Audit Trails**: Implement logging and monitoring of ACL enforcement decisions. Monitoring which ACL rules are being hit and which are being violated can provide insights into potential security issues or misconfigurations.
- **Consistent Updates**: Keep ACLs updated in tandem with changes in client roles or system architecture. Delay in updating ACLs can lead to windows of opportunity for security breaches.

Testing ACL Configurations:

- **Regular Testing**: Regularly test the ACL configurations to ensure they are enforcing the intended policies. This can be done through automated testing scripts that attempt to access various MQTT topics with different client credentials to verify that access controls are working as expected.
- **Change Management**: Incorporate ACL changes into your change management process. Any changes to ACLs should go through the same review and approval processes as other critical system changes to ensure that unintended consequences are identified and mitigated before going live.

Common Pitfalls and How to Avoid Them

- **Lack of Documentation**: Often, ACLs are set up without adequate documentation, leading to confusion and errors during updates. Ensure that all ACL configurations are well-documented, explaining the purpose and scope of each entry.
- **Failure to Remove Old Entries**: As users or services are decommissioned, their corresponding ACL entries might not be updated, leaving unnecessary access rights in the system. Implement a routine check to remove or update deprecated entries.
- **Insecure Default Settings**: Default configurations of some MQTT brokers may not enforce ACLs strictly, potentially leaving the system open to unauthorized access. Always ensure that the broker's default configuration is adjusted to enforce ACLs strictly from the start.

By adhering to these best practices, you can ensure that ACLs are an effective tool in securing your MQTT deployment, facilitating robust access control without adding undue administrative burden as your system evolves.

Advanced ACL Features: Dynamic ACLs

Dynamic Access Control Lists (ACLs) represent a sophisticated approach to managing permissions in MQTT systems, enabling real-time adjustments to ACL entries based on changes in system state, user behavior, or contextual factors. This adaptability enhances security and operational efficiency, particularly in complex or highly dynamic environments.

Understanding Dynamic ACLs

What Are Dynamic ACLs?

- Dynamic ACLs are not static but can change based on predefined rules, events, or conditions. This capability allows MQTT brokers to adapt permissions dynamically, providing or restricting access as necessary without manual intervention.

Benefits of Dynamic ACLs:

- **Flexibility**: They adapt to changes in the environment or user status, such as adjusting permissions based on time of day, user location, or specific events (e.g., triggering higher security protocols during an identified security threat).
- **Enhanced Security**: By adjusting permissions in real-time, dynamic ACLs can minimize potential security risks dynamically, such as limiting access in response to anomalous behavior that might indicate a security breach.
- **Scalability**: They handle changes in user roles and system growth more fluidly, without requiring constant manual updates to ACL entries.

Implementing Dynamic ACLs in MQTT

Real-Time Updates Based on Events:

- Implement mechanisms within the MQTT broker or through integrated services that monitor for specific events or conditions and trigger ACL updates accordingly. For example, an MQTT client's access could be restricted after repeated failed authentication attempts.

Context-Sensitive ACLs:

- Use context-aware security policies that adjust ACLs based on contextual information like user location, connection security level, or device type. For instance, only allow publishing to sensitive topics from devices connected through secured networks.

Integration with External Systems:

- Dynamic ACLs can be managed by integrating the MQTT system with external identity and access management systems (IAM), which maintain user roles and permissions across an enterprise. Changes in the IAM system can propagate in real-time to the MQTT broker's ACLs.

Use of Scripts and Automation:

- Employ scripts or automation tools to modify ACL configurations dynamically. These scripts can be triggered by external monitoring tools or internal events logged by the MQTT broker.

Examples and Technologies

Using MQTT Broker Hooks:

- Some advanced MQTT brokers support programmable hooks that can be used to execute custom scripts or logic when specific events occur. For example, upon a new client connection, a hook could assess the client's credentials against current security policies and dynamically set ACL permissions.

EMQ X ACL Plugin:

- Brokers like EMQ X offer plugins that support dynamic ACLs. The EMQ X ACL plugin can interact with external databases or services in real-time to fetch or update ACL rules based on the current system state or triggered events.

Rule-Based Dynamic ACLs:

- Implement a rule engine that evaluates certain conditions or rules to dynamically adjust ACL entries. For instance, a rule could be set to restrict access to publishing on "control" topics if system load is high, ensuring prioritization of critical communications.

Best Practices

- **Testing and Validation**: Rigorously test dynamic ACL configurations in a controlled environment before deploying them in production to ensure that they behave as expected without unintended side effects.
- **Monitoring and Logging**: Continuously monitor the effects of dynamic ACLs and maintain comprehensive logs of ACL changes and the reasons for those changes. This is crucial for troubleshooting and auditing.
- **Security Assessment**: Regularly assess the security implications of dynamically changing ACLs to ensure that the mechanisms used to trigger ACL changes do not introduce new vulnerabilities.

Dynamic ACLs offer a powerful way to enhance the adaptability and security of MQTT deployments, making them ideal for environments where user roles, behaviors, and conditions are continually changing.

Appendix A: Glossary of Terms

This glossary provides definitions for key terms and concepts related to MQTT, enhancing understanding and ensuring clarity throughout the book. The terms are listed in alphabetical order.

1. **ACL (Access Control List)**: A list that specifies which clients are authorized to access certain topics on an MQTT broker.
2. **Authentication**: The process of verifying the identity of a client or server.
3. **Authorization**: The process of determining if a client has permission to perform a specific action within the MQTT system.
4. **Bridge**: A connection between two MQTT brokers that allows messages to be passed between them.
5. **Broker**: A server that receives messages from publishing clients and sends them to subscribing clients.
6. **Certificate**: A digital form used in SSL/TLS to verify the identity of a client or server.
7. **Clean Session**: A flag in MQTT that specifies whether the broker should retain information about a client after it disconnects.
8. **Client**: A device or application that connects to an MQTT broker to send or receive messages.
9. **Connection**: The link established between an MQTT client and broker over which messages are exchanged.
10. **DISCONNECT Packet**: An MQTT message sent by a client to indicate

that it wishes to disconnect from the broker.

11. **Encryption**: The process of encoding messages to prevent unauthorized access.

12. **Endpoint**: A specific destination or origin within an MQTT network, such as a client or broker.

13. **Keep Alive**: A mechanism used to ensure that the connection between the client and the broker is still open.

14. **Last Will and Testament**: An MQTT message that is specified at connection time and sent by the broker if the client disconnects ungracefully.

15. **Message**: Data transmitted between clients and the broker.

16. **MQTT**: Message Queuing Telemetry Transport, a protocol designed for lightweight communications between devices.

17. **Payload**: The content of an MQTT message.

18. **Persistent Session**: A session where the broker stores all subscriptions and messages for a client across connections.

19. **PINGREQ and PINGRESP**: MQTT messages used to check the connection between the client and broker.

20. **Port**: A numerical value used to identify specific processes or services on a network.

21. **Protocol**: A set of rules governing the exchange or transmission of data between devices.

22. **Publish/Subscribe**: A messaging pattern where senders (publishers) do not program the messages to be sent directly to specific receivers (subscribers).

23. **QoS (Quality of Service)**: A level that guarantees the delivery of MQTT messages:

   - **0**: At most once delivery.
   - **1**: At least once delivery.
   - **2**: Exactly once delivery.

1. **Retained Messages**: MQTT messages that are saved by the broker to

be sent to future subscribers of a topic.

2. **SSL/TLS (Secure Sockets Layer/Transport Layer Security)**: Protocols that provide security over a computer network.

3. **Subscriber**: A client that receives messages from a broker based on topic subscriptions.

4. **Subscription**: The act of a client requesting to receive messages from specific topics.

5. **Topic**: The label attached to an MQTT message, which determines how the message is distributed by the broker.

6. **Unsubscribe**: The act of a client indicating that it no longer wants to receive messages from specific topics.

7. **Username/Password**: Credentials used by a client to authenticate with a broker.

8. **Wildcard**: Special characters (+ and #) used in topic filters to allow subscriptions to multiple topics at once.

9. **Will Flag**: A flag that specifies whether a client has defined a Last Will and Testament message.

10. **Will Message**: See Last Will and Testament.

11. **Will QoS**: The Quality of Service level with which the Will Message is to be published.

12. **Will Retain**: A flag indicating if the Will Message should be retained by the broker.

Appendix B: MQTT Command Reference

This appendix provides a concise reference guide to common MQTT commands used in the protocol's operations. It details essential commands such as connecting, subscribing, publishing, and disconnecting, serving as a practical resource for developers working with MQTT.

CONNECT

- **Description**: Initiates a connection between an MQTT client and a broker.
- **Usage**: The CONNECT command is the first packet sent by the client to the server. It contains the client identifier, username, password, Will message, and other flags.
- **Example**:

```python
import paho.mqtt.client as mqtt

def on_connect(client, userdata, flags, rc):
    print("Connected with result code "+str(rc))

client = mqtt.Client()
client.on_connect = on_connect
client.connect("mqtt.example.com", 1883, 60)
client.loop_start()
```

PUBLISH

- **Description**: Sends a message from the client to the broker, which then forwards it to subscribing clients.
- **Usage**: The PUBLISH command is used to send messages to a specified topic, which subscribers to that topic will receive.
- **Example**:

```
client.publish("home/temperature", "23°C")
```

SUBSCRIBE

- **Description**: Subscribes the client to one or more topics to receive messages published to those topics.
- **Usage**: The SUBSCRIBE command is sent by the client to the broker to request messages from specific topics.
- **Example**:

```
def on_message(client, userdata, message):
    print(f"Received message '{message.payload.decode()}'
on topic '{message.topic}'")

client.subscribe("home/temperature")
client.on_message = on_message
```

UNSUBSCRIBE

- **Description**: Stops the client from receiving messages from specified topics.
- **Usage**: The UNSUBSCRIBE command is used by the client to stop receiving messages on specific topics previously subscribed to.
- **Example**:

```
client.unsubscribe("home/temperature")
```

DISCONNECT

- **Description**: Ends an MQTT session between the client and the broker.
- **Usage**: The DISCONNECT command is sent by the client to notify the broker that it wishes to close the connection.
- **Example**:

```
client.disconnect()
```

PINGREQ and PINGRESP

- **Description**: Keeps the connection alive between the client and the broker.
- **PINGREQ (Ping Request)**: Sent by the client to check if the server is responsive.
- **PINGRESP (Ping Response)**: Sent by the server in response to a

PINGREQ.

- **Usage**: These commands are used primarily to ensure that the network connection between the client and the broker remains active and to prevent timeouts.
- **Example**:

```
# Handled automatically by most MQTT client libraries
```

This command reference serves as a quick guide for developers implementing MQTT protocols, detailing the basic operations necessary for effective MQTT communication.

Appendix C: Tools and Resources for MQTT Development

This appendix offers a comprehensive list of tools, software, books, and online resources essential for developers working with MQTT. It includes broker software, client libraries, testing tools, books, training resources, and community platforms.

MQTT Broker Software

Mosquitto

- **Description**: An open-source MQTT broker known for its simplicity and effectiveness in both testing and production environments.
- **Website**: https://mosquitto.org/

EMQ X

- **Description**: A scalable, open-source MQTT broker designed for high-throughput scenarios and extensive IoT applications.
- **Website**: https://www.emqx.io/

HiveMQ

- **Description**: A robust commercial MQTT broker that supports large-scale deployments and integrates extensive plugins.
- **Website**: https://www.hivemq.com/

Client Libraries

Paho MQTT

- **Description**: Provides scalable open-source client implementations in various programming languages including Python, Java, C, and JavaScript.
- **Website**: https://www.eclipse.org/paho/

MQTT.js

- **Description**: A leading MQTT client for Node.js, suitable for server-side and browser-based applications.
- **Website**: https://github.com/mqttjs/MQTT.js

Testing Tools

MQTT.fx

- **Description**: A graphical testing tool that facilitates debugging of MQTT client setups, subscriptions, and message publications.
- **Website**: https://mqttfx.jensd.de/

MQTT Explorer

- **Description**: Provides a comprehensive view of MQTT topics, aiding in the debugging and analysis of MQTT environments.
- **Website**: http://mqtt-explorer.com/

Books and Training Resources

"Mastering MQTT" by Tim Grossmann

- **Description**: This book covers various aspects of MQTT, from basic to advanced, providing real-world examples and case studies.
- **Availability**: Available on major bookselling platforms.

HiveMQ MQTT Essentials

- **Description**: A blog series that delves into the fundamentals of MQTT, ideal for beginners.
- **Website**: https://www.hivemq.com/tags/mqtt-essentials/

Udemy Courses on MQTT

- **Description**: Various courses on MQTT for all skill levels, from basics to building IoT applications using MQTT.
- **Website**: https://www.udemy.com/courses/search/?q=mqtt

Community and Learning Platforms

MQTT.org

- **Description**: The official website for MQTT protocol, offering specifications, forums, and developer resources.
- **Website**: https://mqtt.org/

Stack Overflow

- **Description**: A vital resource for troubleshooting and community support, with numerous discussions and solutions related to MQTT.
- **Website**: https://stackoverflow.com/questions/tagged/mqtt

These tools and resources provide a solid foundation for anyone involved in developing, deploying, and managing MQTT-based applications, supporting a wide range of needs from learning and development to professional implementation.

www.ingramcontent.com/pod-product-compliance
Lightning Source LLC
LaVergne TN
LVHW041203050326
832903LV00020B/428